From the painting by N. C. Wyeth

THE BOY CHRIST IN THE CARPENTER'S SHOP

HOW ONE MAN
CHANGED THE WORLD

*A Story Told for Boys and Girls
with Questions and Topics
for Study*

FERDINAND Q. BLANCHARD

THE PILGRIM PRESS

BOSTON   CHICAGO

TO

VIRGINIA
FOR WHOM THIS WAS WRITTEN
THAT SHE MIGHT KNOW AND UNDERSTAND

CONTENTS

PREFACE

The contents of this little book were first prepared to tell one little girl the most important story in the world. I hope other children may discover in it the interest she did. But from time to time some older people may turn its pages. For them this preface is written.

There will be those who will protest at once that some most important things are left unsaid in the narrative which follows. The charge is freely admitted. It was no part of my purpose to teach any of the doctrines the Christian Church has developed regarding Jesus. I have had in mind a much simpler, but, as I see it, an equally important task. Jesus appeared to his generation as a young man within the normal framework of human life of that day. When his followers meditated afterwards upon what he had been and done, they were led to certain conclusions concerning him. How far they were correct in their thinking is one of the central questions of the Christian world today. But whatever one decides, there is surely gain in knowing the facts of the life in the simple form in which they made their appeal.

It was because I found children likely to begin speaking of Jesus with some theological statement which they had been taught, but whose meaning they did not at all grasp, and because their knowledge

seemed too often to end with this same inadequately understood statement, that I have desired to make him
seem as real a personality as Abraham Lincoln, or as
Jesus himself seems when one walks over the very hills
he climbed and stands by the lake beside which he
spoke his truth.

I would not claim that I am doing what no one has
ever done before. Many books have set forth with
picturesque detail the customs of his day and the sort
of country in which he lived. But, so far as I happen
to know, the Lives of Christ which do this fall into one
of two groups. Those of one sort, which raise none or
few of the critical questions centering about the New
Testament narratives, permit the beliefs of a later
time deeply to color the picture. Those of another sort
present not the story of a life but essentially a discussion
of the questions raised by Jesus' career and character
and the existing records. A simple narrative, as
Farrar, for example, set it down, but told with full
recognition of the conclusions of modern scholarship,
I have not personally seen.

To tell the story thus, and so that a child might understand it was my aim. How far the end has been
attained, it is for those who read what follows to say.

I am indebted to my friend, the Reverend Charles
Campbell, a companion in a visit to Palestine, for per-
mission to use photographs which he took on that
occasion as the basis of the illustrations in the book.

I would also express my appreciation to my assistant

in my church, Miss, Louise Harper, for carefully
reading the manuscript and suggesting certain changes
to make the story clearer for the children.

The appearance of a second edition of this little
book gives me an opportunity to thank the many
friends whose interest in and approval of it have been
a reward beyond what I had dared to hope. Certain
of their concrete suggestions have been embodied in
this edition.

One use of the book which was not anticipated has
been its inclusion here and there in church school cur-
ricula. This suggested the preparation of a set of
questions for each chapter which would serve as a
definite basis of study. They have been prepared by
Charlotte Chambers Jones and will be found to be
most happily adapted to the end in view.

FERDINAND Q. BLANCHARD

Euclid Avenue Congregational Church
Cleveland, Ohio

How One Man Changed the World

CHAPTER I

THE HOME AT NAZARETH

IF you should go aboard a modern steamship in the harbor of New York and travel for a week across the Atlantic Ocean, you could finally sail between two points of land, one in Europe and one in Africa, and come into the Mediterranean Sea. Then for at least five days more you could travel still farther east over its blue waters, until at last you would come in sight of a long stretch of hills running from north to south. The country towards which you were drawing near would strike you as a land of hills, climbing up and up towards the sky.

It is not a very big land. From north to south its length is not over one hundred and fifty miles. From the shore of the Mediterranean going straight east, you could easily ride across it during one afternoon in an automobile, for the distance is only about fifty miles. There is only one large city. The towns are a good way apart. There is but one river and that, the Jordan, bounds the land on the east. Much of the year the country looks bare and brown because there is little rain. But the land draws people to visit it from every corner of the earth, because *there* was born the man whose life has been of more importance to our lives than that of any other man who ever lived.

His father's name was Joseph and his mother's name was Mary. They lived in a town up among some great hills in the northern part of Palestine. It has been thought that their little boy was born in a small city called Bethlehem, some seventy miles away towards the south, where they had gone on a journey. We do not know surely about this. Nobody thought when he was a boy that he was going to be so famous when he grew up, and his parents were poor people whose doings were not especially noticed by others. After he became very well known, all sorts of stories were told — some of them very beautiful stories about angels and wise, rich men who came to see him. But these stories only help us to see how much people had grown to love him. We know that whether or not he was actually born in Nazareth, that is the place where his parents lived and that is where he grew up as a boy. He was named Jesus. People then had but one name usually.

The town of Nazareth was in a beautiful location. One has but to walk a little way beyond its buildings to have a view over far reaches of level plain and low hills and high mountains. When as a boy Jesus climbed the hill behind the village, he would see just below where he stood a wide green stretch of country across which, like a waving line of brown, stretched a road. On this road he would see merchants and soldiers, camels and horses, wagons and chariots, people on pleasure and others on business, going and coming from early morning until the shadows fell over the hills, and Nazareth people lighted their lamps and began to think of going to bed.

There is a story that once he went to Jerusalem, a long, long journey on foot it was, for a great celebration. There he became so interested in what was going on and in talking with people in the great church called the temple, that his father and mother lost him in the crowd. Thinking that he must be with some of their neighbors, they started home without him and then had to go back and search for him. You may be sure they were glad to find him safe and sound.

After a while other children came into the home. There were four brothers and two sisters. As their house was a small one, we can be sure it was a busy, merry place with nine people in it. The children went to school where they learned to read and write. But most of all they studied what we call the Old Testament. This was the history of their land and full of many things their famous men had said. So it was a very important book to know. Every boy, at least, had to study it hard and long.

When school was over they played games in the streets, or climbed over the hill on whose side the town was built, and very certainly they took turns helping their mother bring home water from the spring whence all their supply came. Sometimes, too, their father wanted their help, and they learned something of his trade as a builder of houses and a maker of all sorts of things from wood.

One sad day Joseph died. He left his family his good name and he left to his oldest boy, Jesus, the task of carrying on the business and earning money for their support. Thus for many years Jesus worked through long days building and repairing houses in Nazareth. He was trusted by his friends and neighbors, and we may be sure he did good work. He seldom went away from home except when he went to Jerusalem for the great feast of the Passover, as I told you he did at least once as a boy. But finally came a time when he said goodbye to his old home forever. How he came to do this we must now discover.

QUESTIONS AND TOPICS FOR STUDY

How should you like to take a journey? First find a globe or a map of the world, and we will start. Can you locate the place where you live? How would you go from there to New York? From there trace a route across the Atlantic Ocean, through the Strait of Gibraltar, into the Mediterranean Sea, and on eastward until you see before you a strip of land stretching north and south. This is Palestine. Can you find a map of this country? (Are there maps in your Bible, or in your lesson books?)

What do you know about Palestine? How large a country is it? How many lakes or seas are there in it? How many rivers? What are the seas and rivers called? Is it a fertile country? Is it rocky and barren? Is it like the desert? How would you describe it to one who had never heard of it? (Study your map carefully for further ideas.)

Why is Palestine of special interest to us? Where did Jesus live?
Where is he supposed to have been born? Why? Who were his
parents? What are some of the special things we remember about
Jesus?

What do you think Jesus may have been like as a boy? Why did
his neighbors not suspect how great he was to become? What may
some of them have thought of him? What might they have thought
of his parents? Why? Do you think the neighbors paid much
attention to this family? What kind of stories grew up about Jesus
after he became famous? What do these stories help us to know
about him?

Where is Nazareth? What kind of surroundings has it? What
mountains are near-by? How far is it from the water? What was
the name of the nearest body of water? What was behind the
town? What could Jesus see from there? What might he have
noticed along the road? (Look up Nazareth and its surroundings
on your map.)

What happened when Jesus first went to Jerusalem? How many
brothers and sisters did he have? What might he have learned at
school? What study of ours would the Old Testament be like?
What did the children do when school was over?

After his father died, what did Jesus do to help his family?
What kind of workman do you think he was? Where did he go
every year? What did he finally do?

Further Discoveries

What did Jesus learn about the feast of the Passover? (Look up
Exodus 12:2, 3, 6, 11, 14-21, 24-28.) What did he learn about
Jehovah or God? (Read Deuteronomy 6:4-9.) What was he
taught about one's neighbor? (See Leviticus 19:18a.) What did
he teach others about this later? (Mark 12:28-34.) How do we
know that as a boy he was interested in thinking about these things?
(Luke 2:41-51.) What did Jesus learn from the law of Moses?
(Exodus 20:3-17.) What was the typical Jewish attitude toward
this law? (Joshua 1:8.) What do we know about Jesus growing
up as a boy? (Luke 2:40, 50.) What Psalms may he have heard

the pilgrims singing as they went up to Jerusalem to keep the Passover? (Turn to Psalm 122, and 24: 1-5, noticing especially verses 3 and 4 of the latter.) What did Jesus say later about the pure in heart seeing God? (Matthew 5: 8.)

Something to Do

How should you like to keep a diary, imagining yourself to be a friend of Jesus in Nazareth? What games might you play together? (See Luke 7: 32.) What did you see Jesus do to help his parents? What did you learn at the synagogue school together? Where did you go with Jesus and the others once a year, after you were twelve? What else will you tell about in your diary? What kind of map could you make for it? What pictures can you find for illustrations? (Ask somebody to help you find these in magazines, such as the *National Geographic,* or in lesson study materials.)

CHAPTER II

A Visit to a Strange Man and What Came of It

THE river Jordan is the east boundary of Palestine. It starts its journey among mountains, but it drops down lower and lower on its way through a deep gorge until it is many, many feet lower than the coast and sea. The country along its banks has no homes upon it and no crops are raised there. It is just bleak bare land except where, close to the water, green grass and rushes grow. And yet it is not very far distant from Jerusalem and smaller towns situated in fertile country.

One day when Jesus had grown to be a young man thirty years old, there suddenly appeared by the bank of the river a very strange-looking man. He had lived by himself without shelter, getting his food as he could from the wild fruits of the hills, and dressing in poor rough clothes made from the skins of camels. But he could speak so interestingly that the few people he first met soon grew into great crowds that wanted to hear him. They called him "John, the Baptizer," because his name was John and because he asked the people who wanted to follow him to be baptized. This was done as a sign that they would try to live good clean lives as he told them to do, so making themselves ready for a new kind of ruler to be sent by God himself to the people.

7

Far away in his hilltown of Nazareth, Jesus heard of this man, of his wonderful speeches and of the crowds of people going to hear him. The time had come when Jesus was able to leave his work and go away from home. His younger brothers had grown up and they could easily care for the family as Jesus had long been doing. So he made up his mind that he would go to see and hear John.

There was another reason. All through these years when Jesus had been living quietly at Nazareth he had been thinking of the way other people lived. He had studied the teaching of the great men who had lived in his country, but he had been thinking things over by himself too. Especially he had thought about God. As the birds circled about in the sky over his head, as the flowers came out in lovely forms and colors on the hillsides each spring, as he had seen the farmers sow the seed and then months later cut down the waving grain, as the crimson and gold of the sunset sky marked the long day's ending, he had seemed to hear God speaking to him of the goodness and care which surrounded everything. And then God seemed to tell him of the love which in a yet greater way was about children and men and women; so that if any of them asked for help to do the right things day by day, God would give it. Jesus was as sure of all this as he was that Nazareth was built on its great hilltop. He wanted other people to be sure, too.

Then he had been noticing how many times people

treated other people unkindly. Rich people thought
they were better than poor people. Perhaps because
in Jesus' home there was little money, he had known
just how unkind this way of acting could be. On the
other hand he saw how much everyone could do to
help make life more pleasant for all the people in
Nazareth.

So it was that Jesus decided that he would tell people what he had come to know. Up to this time he had
had no opportunity; but at last, he was free to do so.
And the things that John the Baptizer did and said
led him, as we shall now see, to begin his own teaching.

From Nazareth Jesus journeyed down on foot to
the place in the Jordan valley where John was to be
found. Perhaps there went with him some other
young men who lived at Capernaum, thirty miles
away over the hills and by the Lake of Galilee. If they
did not go with him, at least they met him when he
reached the end of the journey. It is worth remember-
ing this, for we shall hear about them later.

Jesus listened to John for several days. Then one
day John was baptizing some of those who had heard
him speak. They wished to show how truly they believed in what he said about right living, how sorry
they were for doing wrong things, and how ready they
were to prepare for the day when someone from God
might come to rule the land. Jesus joined this company and went down into the water of the Jordan to
be baptized.

It was while this was occurring that something happened to Jesus which was very important. Later, he told the young men who became his daily companions about it. He said that it seemed as though God spoke to him, and the words he seemed to hear were, "You are my dear son; I am pleased with what you are doing."

Have you ever done something because you knew you ought to do it, and have you ever "felt right," as we say, after doing it? Your conscience told you that you had done right. Something like that happened to Jesus; only it was an experience much more clear, sure, and definite than comes to us, because the thing Jesus had decided to do was so much more important than what we have to decide to do. Jesus told about this as though people might have seen and heard what went on in his own heart; or perhaps those who wrote about it later heard the story in that way. At any rate, that is the way the story stands in the New Testament today. But what it really means is that Jesus knew that the things he had come to believe were indeed right and true, and that his decision to tell other people was the decision God wanted him to make.

QUESTIONS AND TOPICS FOR STUDY

Look up on your map the Jordan River. In what mountain does it have its source? What course does it take? What kind of channel has it? Through what countries does it flow? What is the land like along its banks? How near does it flow to Jerusalem?

See in how many different ways you can describe "John the

Baptizer." What did Jesus hear about John? Why did Jesus
decide to go to see him? What had Jesus thought about God?
Why did he wish to tell his thoughts to others? What had he
noticed about the different ways people had of treating one another?

How did Jesus get to the place where John was? Who else went?
What did Jesus do when John was baptizing some of his hearers?
Why do you think Jesus was happy to be baptized with the others?
Of what may he have been thinking?

Why did Jesus believe God was pleased with the decision he had
made that day? Can you think of something you once did which
you felt would please your parents? How did you feel after
doing it?

Further Discoveries

How was John dressed? (See Matthew 3:4.) Was this the
usual costume of a prophet? (2 Kings 1:8.) What is meant by
"hairy"? (Zechariah 13:4.) Find in one of the prophets a pas-
sage of which John's hearers might have thought as they listened
to him. (Isaiah 40:3-5.) How did John try to prepare the way
for the coming of God's kingdom? (Luke 3:10, 11.) What did
he say to the tax collectors? (Luke 3:12, 13.) What did John
think of Jesus? (Matthew 3:11, 13-15.)

Something to Do

Make believe you were with the crowd, listening to John preach.
What will you say in your diary about his looks, his message, and
what happened when Jesus came?

CHAPTER III

AN IMPORTANT BATTLE

BETWEEN the Jordan valley, where the people had gathered to hear John, and the city of Jerusalem, lies one of the wildest bits of country upon which the eye of man ever rests. There is not a blade of green grass or a suggestion of human life in the whole region. When one looks over it from the highlands about Jerusalem, it seems like a great ocean of rolling hills and valleys, which even in the bright Syrian sun is so waste and bare as to bring to you a feeling of great loneliness. If Jesus wanted to be alone, as he did, no place in the world would give a better opportunity. He had but to walk a few hours from the people gathered in John's company, to lose himself in this wilderness of rolling country, and there he could be by himself to think about the meaning of the life which he was now going to undertake. Sure that it was his mission to go out and tell the people what he believed about God and their conduct towards one another, the question he had to decide was how he should do this. There was one way which would naturally make its appeal to Jesus' mind.

The whole country was excited with the idea that a leader was coming to them in some strange, wonderful way, to rule as their king in Jerusalem. Both before and after the time when Jesus lived, men who had summoned the people to follow them, promising

release from the rule of the Roman Empire which had
conquered the country, always succeeded in getting
followers. Even when they were arrested and punished by the Romans, the people admired them. Now
if Jesus told the people he was such a leader, he was
sure of securing their interest.

On the other hand, there was danger lest the very
thing he wanted them to believe would be forgotten
as they dreamed and talked of armies and battles and
palaces. Still it was the easy way to stir up enthusiasm,
and the question would naturally be whether it was
not, therefore, the best thing to do at the beginning.

As of his experience in the baptism, so what happened in those lonely days on the desolate hills could
only have been known by what Jesus told at some later
time. And like what happened at the Jordan, so in this
case the best way he could tell about it was in what we
call figurative language. That is to say, he described
what was going on in his mind as though it were something that one could have seen had he been there. He
told of a kind of contest between himself and a strange,
terrible creature called the "Spirit of Evil," or the
"Devil." Jesus was very hungry and the creature tells
him to turn the stones into bread. Then he seems to
take Jesus up to one of the tall towers of the temple at
Jerusalem and he bids Jesus throw himself down, so as
to show that God will not let him be hurt. Finally
they seem to stand on a high mountain, looking over
all the world, and the creature says that Jesus shall be

able to rule over everything just by bowing down and worshiping him.

Now we have to ask what these pictures mean, because really there was no evil creature there with Jesus. They did not go to the temple. There is no mountain from which one can see even the whole of Palestine. It is not very easy for boys and girls to understand, but unless they do understand it they cannot understand Jesus. Just as you are tempted by bad thoughts, bad desires, so Jesus was tempted. And the bad thing he was tempted to do was to claim to be this sort of great national hero, unlike all other men, whom God would care for and protect better than he did other men.

Jesus conquered in this battle; that is, he got the better of all these bad desires. He made up his mind that he would go about quietly telling people about God and how they might live, and he would not show himself to be different from others, except as he trusted God more fully and did right things every day. This took courage, as we shall see. The other way looked easy. This way Jesus knew would be very, very hard. But in those lonely days in the wilderness he made the great resolve from which he never turned back, even though we shall find it meant pain and hardship and at last death.

QUESTIONS AND TOPICS FOR STUDY

Turn again to your map of Palestine. Trace the Jordan River until you come to the part opposite Jerusalem. What is the country like here, between the river and Jerusalem? How does it appear from Jerusalem? Why would it be a good place for anyone who wished to be alone? How long would it take Jesus to reach this wilderness? From where did he start? Why did Jesus wish to go to this deserted part of the country? What did he believe his real work was to be? How would he be able to make people listen to his message?

What kind of leader were the Jewish people waiting for? Why did they want a king of their own? What had happened to some of their leaders who had tried to help the people break away from the Roman rule?

What might have happened if Jesus had started his work as one of these leaders? Why would the people have listened eagerly to what he had to say? What was he afraid they might be interested in? What did he want them to be interested in?

How did Jesus describe what took place in his mind, as he thought of going about his work? Who was the one he said tempted him to appear as the promised savior of his people? How did the people of that day think of the spirit of evil? Was it something very real to them? Why?

What were the three things the spirit of evil seemed to tell Jesus to do? Why would people come to hear somebody who could turn stones into the round flat loaves of bread they ate in Palestine? What would everybody think if Jesus jumped off a tower of the temple and remained uninjured? How might one win a great following by serving the spirit of evil? Which of these three temptations do you think might have been the hardest for Jesus to refuse? Why? Can you think of similar temptations that come to people today? Why is it necessary to overcome them?

What did Jesus finally decide to do? Why would he be like other people? How would he be different? Could others learn to be different in that way also?

Which way of leading the people would take the greatest courage? Why? Did Jesus ever turn back? What would be the result of keeping to his decision?

Further Discoveries

Who else went into a quiet place to think over his problems of leadership? (Exodus 34: 4, 27, 28.) Had Jesus ever heard of this? Read about another ancient prophet who sought a mountain in order to commune with God. (I Kings 19: 8, 9.) You will notice that Moses, Elijah, and Jesus stayed in the mountains of the wilderness for forty days without food. Forty was a general number meaning a great many. Why do you think Jesus may have wished to pattern after Moses and Elijah? How famous were these two prophets of the Old Testament? (If you do not know, see if you can find out.) How can we find help in solving some of our difficult problems? How familiar was Jesus with the writings of his people? (Psalm 91 : 11, 12; Deuteronomy 8: 3; 6: 16 and 6: 13.) How can wise commands or good advice often help us in time of temptation? Where can we find such rules of living? Can you think of some that are helpful to you now? Find some that you would like to learn. (Ask somebody to help you find good ones.)

Something to Do

Write a story about a boy or a girl who was tempted to cheat in a game or in schoolwork, in order to win applause, and what happened. Continue your diary, making believe you heard Jesus tell his friends about his experience in the wilderness.

CHAPTER IV

A Bad Man's Evil Deed

WHEN Jesus came back from those lonely days in the wild country it was not clear what he would do next. "Why did he not begin speaking to people?" you may ask. Because he did not want to do anything that might hurt John. If he had begun gathering people about him he might have drawn them away from John. Jesus was too kind, too considerate to do that, so he seems to have lived very quietly for a while. It is possible he was in Nazareth going about his work again as a builder. But, alas for John! Jesus did not have very long to wait in this way. There was a bad and cruel prince who ruled over a part of Palestine. John spoke very boldly of the evil things this prince had done. The prince sent some of his soldiers, and they arrested John and shut him up in a dungeon in a gloomy castle.

It was dark and damp. No friend was able to help him, for the prince was too strong. John was kept there for some months. One day there was a party at the court of this bad prince, and one of the guests, a young girl, danced. The prince was so pleased that he told her he would give her anything she wanted. This was such a great opportunity to get some wonderful present that before telling the prince what she wished, the girl talked it over with her mother. If one did not know what terrible things people do when they are

angry and hate other people, one could not believe
it to be true that her mother suggested to her what she
did. For the girl went to the prince and asked — what
do you suppose? — that John be put to death.

The reason the mother of the girl told her to ask for
this was because she hated John. She had married the
prince after both she and he had done many bad things.
And John had spoken about it publicly. This it was
that made her so angry, and her rage was all the greater
because she knew he had spoken truly.

The prince, bad man that he was, did not want to
do the terrible thing the girl asked him. But he had
promised and he made the excuse that he must keep
his promise. Of course, one ought to keep a promise,
but when keeping it means doing something thor-
oughly wrong without any good reason, the law of
doing right sets aside the law of keeping one's promise.
The prince had done wrong in arresting John. He had
been foolish in making his promise. Now he added
the fearful crime of having John murdered to please
his bad wife and foolish daughter. One day in the
gloomy castle the brave John was killed. So died the
man who had influenced Jesus so much that he will
never be forgotten.

I have gone ahead in John's story beyond the point
we had reached in telling what Jesus did. John's death
did not come immediately after he was shut up in
prison. Indeed, he lived long enough for Jesus to become well known and for the news of his deeds and

words to reach into the dungeon, making John wonder if Jesus might not be the very one whose coming he had told the people to expect.

When the news reached Jesus that John could not preach any longer but was shut up in the dungeon, he left his home in Nazareth never to return to it except for a visit. He set out across the hill country for a long walk of thirty miles to reach the busy cities that were built on the shores of the Lake of Galilee. His way led him in and out among the high places of the hill country, by steep paths that tested the strength of every traveler. Finally he came out upon a broad shoulder of the highlands and saw below him the beautiful lake, reflecting the sails of fishing boats. Down to the water at several points ran clustered buildings of little cities, gleaming white. The people looked small indeed from his lofty lookout, but there were, he knew, thousands of them doing business around that quiet sea.

Swiftly the path took him down to the shore. To which of the several cities should he go? He decided upon Capernaum because some young men lived there whom he had met while listening to the preaching of John. Thither he went and passing through the busy streets reached the shore of the lake.

QUESTIONS AND TOPICS FOR STUDY

Why did not Jesus begin at once to preach to the people? How might his preaching have affected John's work? Why do you think

Jesus may have wanted the people to hear what John had to tell them?

What happened to John soon after this? Why did the prince put him into prison? Why did the wife of the prince wish to see John put to death? How do we usually feel toward those who know about our wrongdoing? Do we have any reason for disliking them? What is it? Whose fault is it if we dislike them? Why?

What did Jesus do while John was in prison? Where did he go after leaving Nazareth? Can you find this lake on your map? Why did Jesus wish to go there?

For You to Decide

Suppose you had promised to do something and afterwards found out that you could not keep your promise; what would you do about it? Suppose you promised to do something and then discovered it would harm somebody else if you kept your promise; what would you do? What kind of promises should we make? How can we tell before we make a promise, whether we shall be able to keep it? Should we ever make a promise we are not sure of being able to keep? Write some rules that you would like to follow about making and keeping promises.

Further Discoveries

How did the king feel when he heard the result of his foolish promise? (Mark 6:26.) What do you think it means when it says "for the sake of his oaths"? (Mark 6:23.) Why did the king feel he must keep his promise for the sake of those feasting with him? How much courage did it take to keep this rash promise? How much courage would it have taken not to keep it? What do you think of this king's courage or lack of it? Compare the king with John. (Read what Jesus once said about John, in Matthew 11:7-11.)

Something to Do

Tell in your diary about John's arrest and how Jesus began to take up the work. Draw a map to show the journey Jesus took from the Jordan River to Nazareth and over to the Lake of Galilee.

CHAPTER V

JESUS BEGINS TO PREACH

WHEREVER there are many fish in the water and many people on the land, fishing is a business in which many men are engaged. It was this way about the Lake of Galilee. There were no factories in which great machines made goods of all sorts and employed large numbers of people. There were no large stores. Small shops occupied some people and farming others. Different trades supplied what was needed at home and abroad. But there were no more busy, useful workers than the men who sailed out on the lake in little boats with large nets, drew in the fish, and then sold them in the shops near the shore.

Jesus' friends belonged to this group. They were two pairs of brothers. He knew where to look for them. The best fishing was done in the very early morning, and now, when the sun was high overhead, the fishermen were busy mending their nets that had been torn by rocks or in the rough handling of their work. Their little boats had been run up on the sand. We do not know all that was said. Probably they talked over what had happened since they had last met. Then Jesus told them of his plan to go about telling people what he knew of God, and how people should act towards one another. Then he said to them: "Come after me and I will make you fishers of men." He asked them, that is, to give up their work there on the lake and go about with him, his comrades on the journeys they would take.

What did they say? They said they would do as Jesus asked. Of course, there were plans to make with their father so that he would have someone else to help him in his work. We must remember two other things, also, that will explain why they could decide so quickly. One is that they were not going to leave Capernaum at once. The other is that in that small country of Palestine they would not be going very far away, and they would be returning home from time to time, even after the journeys began. Therefore, it was not necessary to make plans such as might be necessary today if four young men were suddenly to give up their business and homes and start a new way of life.

The thing that most interests us is that Jesus had so won their admiration and love that whatever might be necessary they were ready to do. They had never met anyone so fine and good and splendid as Jesus. In order to help him and to be with him, they were ready to leave all else and follow him.

———————

As Jesus was going to be in Capernaum often, it was necessary to find a place to live. Perhaps he found this at the home of one of these fishermen where he was always a welcome guest. Jesus did not intend to stay for a long while in Capernaum, but it was natural to begin to teach there.

You ask, of course, just what Jesus did and said as

JESUS BEGINS TO PREACH   23

he went about his task of making known to people
what he had come to know. It was very simple. He
would join some group of people, share in their con-
versation and presently begin to speak of the things
he knew to be all important. What he said was so interesting that those who heard him began telling
others about it. Very soon, therefore, when he appeared in any group, people who knew of it made
haste to leave whatever else they might be doing and
to become listeners. Just the fact that he was likely to
speak to them drew ever larger numbers of people together. Finally it became difficult to find a place where
he might speak and be heard by all who desired to
listen.

Sometimes he would get into a little boat and push
out from the shore just far enough so that people gathered for some distance along the pebbly beach could
easily see him. From the boat, as from a platform,
with the background of the blue lake and its encircling
mountains, he would tell them about themselves and
God. At other times he would leave the city and climb
up the slopes of the hills. At some convenient spot with
the people seated on the grass all about him, he would
speak to them. They never grew weary of hearing
him, but as we shall see in a later chapter, sometimes
forgot all about going home until they were all "late
for supper," as we would say.

How do we know what he said? Nowadays it is
possible to take down by what we call "shorthand

writing" everything a speaker says. In the days of Jesus this system was not known. Moreover, no one at first supposed that Jesus was going to be the greatest person in history, so nobody tried to keep a record of his words. But he had a way of speaking that made it easy to remember what he had said. Moreover, when there were no newspapers and very few books, people took pains to remember what they heard. And thus it happened that many of the sayings of Jesus were saved.

He did not teach in any set way, taking up one subject after another like lessons in a schoolbook. Ordinarily, he began to speak of something that he had seen or which had occurred recently, and used this to explain the thing he wanted them to understand. He particularly liked to tell some simple little story which would make clear at once what he wished to say. One day, for example, as he was sitting in a little boat, he saw over the heads of the people on the shore a man walking slowly across a field where the brown soil had been turned by the plow. This man was sowing seed. Perhaps Jesus could see a beaten path at one side of the field and low underbrush along another side. Overhead he could see birds sailing on outstretched wings across the field, now swooping down to the ground, now rising high in the clear bright air.

Of what he saw he made a little story. A man, he said, went out and scattered seed over his field. Some of the seed fell on the beaten path. There the birds saw it and picked it up for food. Other seed fell

where weeds and underbrush choked it as it started
to grow. Still other seed made a start, but the ground
had stones in it and the hot sun withered the seed because it could not send down long roots. But other seed
fell where it took root and grew up into a fine field of
wheat. And, said Jesus, that is just like what happens
to my words. Some people hear and pay no attention.
Some hear and forget. Only a few hear and obey, but
then there comes a harvest of good words and deeds.
It was easy to remember a story or parable, as we have
called it, like that.

When Jesus did not speak in parables he often used
short striking sentences that stuck in the memory. He
said things like these: "You are the salt of the earth
... you are the light of the world ... no man can serve
two masters ... if a man would save his life, let him
lose it." Even when it might not be quite easy to understand exactly what he meant, the things he said
could not be forgotten. If, therefore, you think of
these various things I have spoken of, you can understand how it was possible, years afterward, to set
down with a good deal of accuracy the teachings he
gave from the little boat or the pleasant hillslope or
the quiet room of someone's home.

He told people what sort of man one should be in
order to bring happiness to others and himself. He
should be considerate, sorry for wrong things so that
he would wish to right them, unselfish, eager to be
good, kind, clean in word and deed, helpful in pre-

venting quarrels, willing to bear hard things in order
to do good. A man such as Jesus would have everyone
be should do more than he is forced to do. He should
be generous as well as just. He should not try to " get
even " when someone does him wrong, but should try
to return good for evil.

These are only a few of the things Jesus said. You
must read all he said for yourself. In the book called
the Gospel of Matthew you will find several chapters,
the fifth, sixth, and seventh, made up of these sayings
of Jesus about the " ideal man," that is, the sort we all
ought to try to be. These chapters contain also much
that he said about God. He is like one's father only
much better, wiser and stronger. As the flowers grow
in the field, becoming very beautiful, and the birds
find food and shelter, so every man and woman, boy
and girl, may be sure God's care surrounds each one,
and that he never forgets or overlooks anyone.

QUESTIONS AND TOPICS FOR STUDY

Describe the occupations of the people who lived around the
Lake of Galilee. Why would a fisherman be a strong and useful
worker? When was the best fishing done? When were nets
mended? When did Jesus talk to his fisher friends?

What did he say to them about the work he was planning to do?
Why did he invite them to be his special comrades? Do you think
they were pleased to do this? Why? What plans did they make
about the fishing business? How far away were they going? How
long would they probably stay?

How did Jesus go about his work? Why did people gather about
him to listen? Where did he sometimes go to talk to the people?

What did he tell them about? Why were some of his sayings remembered? How did he often make his meaning clear to the
people? What story did he tell them about a sower? What do we
call that kind of story? What did this one mean? How else did
he teach the people?

How did he say one could be happy and bring happiness to others?
Where in the Bible can you read some of the things he taught? What
did Jesus say God is like? How did Jesus tell of God's care?

Further Discoveries

Find some of the things Jesus told the people. (Matthew 5:
1-12.) How do you think he learned these things? Compare these
sayings with some of the decisions Jesus made in the wilderness.
(Matthew 4: 1-10.) What hunger did Jesus think was most important? (Matthew 4:4 and 5:6.) How would true sons of
God act? (Compare Matthew 4:6, 7, with 5:9.) How might
one inherit the kingdoms of the earth? (Matthew 4:8, 9.) Who
could possess the kingdom of heaven? (Matthew 5: 10.)

Something to Do

Make some rules for daily living, based upon Jesus' teaching as
to how we may be truly happy or blessed. Continue your diary,
as told by one of Jesus' friends. What will you say about fishermen? What about Jesus talking to the people? What story will
you say he told? What rules did he give for living?

CHAPTER VI

JESUS AND THE SICK PEOPLE

THE days and months passed swiftly by, and the fame of Jesus spread ever more widely. For so many of the people were poor and sad, so badly treated by the rich and the powerful, that they found comfort and courage in Jesus' words. But something else helped very much to make him known and to bring people to the place where he was. He made sick people well.

In those days there were few doctors, and such as there were knew very little about the cause or the cure of sickness. People had strange ideas of what made one ill. Nowadays we know that small living things we call "germs" get into the body and cause disease.

Of all that has helped to get rid of much pain and weakness in the world, there was scarcely any knowledge in Jesus' day. People had an idea that evil spirits caused illness. Particularly if anyone had anything the matter with his brain and acted foolishly or wildly, being either as we now say imbecile or insane, he was said to be possessed by a demon. And these poor unhappy people, being told that some demon was inside of them, came to believe it. Thus the patient and his friends alike shared this wrong but sad and terrible idea.

A wonderful thing it seemed when, in a country where sickness thus meant helplessness and hopelessness, there appeared one with the power to make people well. It is impossible to imagine how it would be if every hospital and doctor we know were taken away. But in part we may feel what this would mean, and then what it would mean if suddenly the news was heard that someone had been found whose touch or word brought back health to sick and suffering people.

And this is what Jesus meant. He made many sick people well. Most interesting, perhaps, and attracting most attention, was the way he gave back to a number of poor sufferers who thought they had demons inside of them the sense of being sane and happy once more. We do not know just how he did it. He used no medicine. It seemed to be the case that there was something about his very presence that brought peace and strength to the sick. Health was in his touch; calmness in his word. He made men feel that God was loving and caring for them. In that faith they felt tides of healing going through their bodies. They felt as though bad spirits could have no power over them when Jesus bade them be well; for Jesus had in his character stores of strength and peace and courage beyond what other men have had.

Very quickly the news went abroad of those first sick people who were cured. And then from near and far came those who needed the help which they believed Jesus could give. Those who were so ill that they could not get to Capernaum by themselves were helped thither by their friends. Finally, the crowds grew so great that Jesus had to leave Capernaum. He had healed the sick because he was sorry for them. But he did not want it thought that his work was only to make sick bodies well, and he feared that so much notice was being paid to his cures that his teaching would not be heard. For a little while, therefore, he went away into the high country that surrounds the Lake of Galilee and looks down upon the city of Capernaum.

QUESTIONS AND TOPICS FOR STUDY

What made Jesus' fame spread so far? What did he do besides talk to people? What kind of people did he go among? What ideas did people have about illness? What did they say of the insane?

How did it seem to the sick when they heard about Jesus' help? What did he often do for those who were supposed to have demons? How did he help them? Why was he able to do this? What kind of person can give strength and courage to those in need of it?

What was the result of Jesus' helping the sick? Why had he done this? What did he think more important even than curing men's bodies? What did he do after a while?

Further Discoveries

Find out about some of the first sick people Jesus helped. (Matthew 8: 1-16.) What happened when a person had leprosy? (Leviticus 13: 45, 46.) Did Jesus follow the law of his people? (Leviticus 14: 2.) What was the gift that Moses commanded? (Leviticus 14: 10, 21, 22.) Why did the centurion think

Jesus could heal his servant with a word? (Matthew 8: 8.) What did the centurion think was inside the servant? How would one get rid of evil spirits? (Matthew 10: 1 and 8: 16.) What do you think might have been the matter with one who had an evil spirit? How could such a person be helped?

Something to Do

Continue your diary by adding what you have heard about Jesus' curing sick people.

CHAPTER VII

How One Man Was Made Well

IT was an afternoon in Capernaum by the lake. Jesus had begun to speak to a group of people that had come together in the house where he lived. Others heard about it and came crowding in to listen to him, until the rooms were as full as they could be. Then the people pressed about the doorway so that nobody could pass in or out freely.

As Jesus was speaking under these conditions, four men drew near to the house carrying a fifth who was ill. He lay on a mat which the friends carried, one at each corner. They and he were eager to reach Jesus because they had heard of his curing people and they wished to have him make this man, who was paralyzed, well and strong again. To their surprise and dismay they saw they could not get within sight or sound of Jesus. But they were not to be turned back.

In order to understand what they did you must know something about the houses in Palestine. In the first place they were then, as they are now, very low compared with houses in America. They usually had no second story. The roofs were flat, and it was often possible to get up to them by an outside stairway. These roofs were made of light material, perhaps grass plastered with mud to be water-tight, and it was easy to open up a large hole in them at any point.

The four friends clambered up to the roof of the

house where Jesus was speaking, lifting up after them their sick friend. Here they set to work and opened a space big enough for them to lower through it the sick man on the mat. In the room below, Jesus and those listening to him would have heard the noise but might not have thought it was due to anything unusual. Suddenly, however, the sun came streaming in through the opening, and a moment later the mat with its load rested in front of Jesus.

He did not need anyone to explain matters to him. At once he knew that the man had been brought to be healed, and glancing up he saw the eager faces of the friends peering down through the hole in the roof. So he stopped short in what he was saying and spoke to the sick man.

"My son," he said, using this kind word to address him, "your sins are forgiven."

That seemed like a strange thing to say. Not only was it strange, but some people in the house that day thought it was a wrong thing to say. We shall see a little later who these people were. They thought Jesus should not have said what he did, because they thought nobody but God could forgive sins. Jesus said it for the reason that he was sure God would forgive. He knew so well what God is like that he could say surely how God felt. And when he saw how the people looked at him in surprise or reproof he hastened to say this:

"Do you think that what I have said is not true?

Well, then, in order to show you that God forgives
I will show you that God will cure the man." Then
he turned to the sick man.

"Get up," he said, "fold up your mat and walk to
your home."

And before their eyes, which could hardly believe
what they saw, the man did just what Jesus bade
him do.

Of course, Jesus did not act or speak like this every
time. He knew that this man had done bad things and
that he had fallen sick because he had done wrong.
He knew also that when the friends tried so very hard
to bring him to Jesus, the man must have wanted to
come because he was sorry for what he had done.
Finally he knew that health for the man's body could
not come unless peace came to his heart. The sick
man had to be sure that God would forgive him and
be his friend before he could feel himself strong and
well once more. So in healing him Jesus was able to
teach that we can always be sure that God is not our
enemy but is like one's father who, when one is sorry
for doing wrong, will help one to be good.

QUESTIONS AND TOPICS FOR STUDY

Where was Jesus one afternoon at Capernaum? What was he
doing? How many were about him? Who came to the house?
Why could they not go inside easily? What did they do to reach
Jesus?

Do you think the people were surprised to see the sick man low-
ered? What did they expect to happen? Why did some think Jesus

had said something wrong? Why did Jesus say it? What did he
mean by it? What did he say to the sick man after that? What
happened? Why did it help the man to know he was forgiven?
How do you feel when your father forgives you after you have
done wrong?

Something to Do

Find this story in the Bible. (Mark 2: 1-12.)

Ask your chum to help you write out a dramatization of it. Perhaps you could act it out with your friends, each adding suggestions
until it is the way you think it should be. What hymn could you
sing after this? Could you also write a prayer to use with it?
Where could you use all this as a special part of some service?

It might be outlined in three parts as follows:

1. Two friends meet and talk about Jesus, wondering if he
could cure their sick friend. A third joins them and says that Jesus
is in a house near-by, talking to the people. They begin to plan how
they might carry the sick man to this place, and decide to call a
fourth to help. The fourth is summoned and agrees to help. They
all go out.

2. The four friends enter, bearing the sick man on a heavy mat.
They caution one another to be careful and go easily. At seeing the
crowd about the door of the house they had hoped to enter they are
dismayed and wonder if they will have to go back again after all
their trouble. One suggests that they find a way, and they think
of several, finally deciding to go up to the roof and make an opening in it.

3. The four friends are seen looking down through the roof,
from the outside, describing what is happening. The door opens
below and through the crowd there comes the sick man, now carrying his mat and praising God. The crowd follows, pushing to get
a look at him, and all express amazement, as well as praise to God
for healing him.

CHAPTER VIII

Jesus' Friends and Enemies

JESUS' words and deeds did two things. They made some people ready to follow him anywhere. They made other people dislike him greatly. We can easily see why the first thing happened. We should expect it to be true. Many men and women, the names of some of whom are set down for us in the New Testament, went where he went whenever they could and told others what helpful things he said, what great cures he worked, and what a wonderful man he was.

It seemed well to Jesus to choose out of this large number of friends a small group who could be with him every day. By hearing him speak and seeing what he did, they from time to time could go to towns he could not visit, carry there his words, and act in his name. Then as time went on and Jesus began to fear that the people who did not like him would not let him teach any more, he wanted to depend upon these special friends of his to carry on what he had begun. We have seen how he had already asked certain young men to be his companions in what he was trying to do. Their names are easy to remember — Peter and Andrew, James and John.

Perhaps none of the larger group except these four were fishermen. One young man was collecting taxes; that is, the money which the Roman people made the Jews pay to them every year. Of the others we know

nothing before they joined Jesus. The young tax col-
lector was called Matthew. These are the names of
the rest: Philip, Bartholomew, Thomas, Thaddeus,
Simon, another James whose father was named Al-
pheus, and last of all, Judas. Although you may forget many of these, be sure you do not forget that last
name, for we shall hear it again.

This group came to be known as "The Twelve."
If you counted you know why the name was given.
Some of them, the first four especially, were more
useful to Jesus than others. But the fact that they all
were with Jesus day after day and knew him better
than anyone else did, made them well known and gave
them at last a special place in people's minds. Many a
night they spent with him on the hills, camping out,
as we should say today. Many an hour he spent with
them alone helping them to see what was true about
God and how one person should act towards another.
They all loved him at first. All loved him to the end
of his short life, except one. The sad story of that one
we shall hear later. They often failed to see what he
wanted them to understand. They made mistakes.
But save that one, Judas, they did the best they could
to be his loyal friends.

I said we are not surprised at their action. But why
did Jesus have enemies? He was always doing good
things. What reason could anyone find to dislike him
and to do him harm? In order to understand this, you
must know a little more about life in Palestine in those

days. There was one group of people in particular known as Pharisees. We do not have any group like them in America, or England, or any other modern country. It was somewhat as though one of our political parties, Republicans or Democrats, was combined with one of our church groups. They were patriotic and religious, eager to help their country and to support what was their church. In many ways, there were no better people in all the land.

But Jesus saw that they were guilty of two great faults. For one thing they looked down upon other people as being not as good as they were. They had a right to think so but not a right to treat other people badly as they seem to have done. In the next place, they had come to the point of thinking that goodness depended on such things as washing at certain times and praying at certain times. Now the things they made so much of were many of them all right. They were intended to help people to be good. But doing them was in itself neither good nor bad. And the Pharisees missed sight of real goodness by talking so much of these ways of being good. In other words, they grew to speak and act as though it were more important to keep one of their customs than to be brave, kind, honorable, and faithful to duty. So Jesus had to point out their mistake and he was disliked by them because he did so. They began to speak disagreeably about him. They tried to turn people against him. They did what they could to hurt and hinder him.

QUESTIONS AND TOPICS FOR STUDY

How did Jesus affect different people? Why did he choose certain ones to be his special friends? Who were the first of these? What was their former work? What did another one of Jesus' friends do? What was his name? Who were the others? How many were there in all? Who is usually named last? Who were the most useful friends to Jesus? Why were they with him so much? What were some of the things they did together? Were they all loyal friends?

Why did Jesus have enemies? What special group disliked him? Who were they? With what were they concerned? What were some of their mistakes? Why did they so insist upon little details? What did they often miss because of this? Why did they dislike Jesus? (Compare this reason with the one we discovered about the king's disliking John.) What did they do to show their dislike? Do you think that kept Jesus from saying what he thought was right? Why not?

Further Discoveries

Find some of the things Jesus said to his followers about bearing hardship for their beliefs. (Matthew 5 : 10-12.) Find some advice about being helpful. (Matthew 5 : 13-16.) Did Jesus believe in the law of his people? (Matthew 5 : 17-19.) What did Jesus think was as bad as murder? (Matthew 5 : 21, 22.) Read an ancient law of justice. (Exodus 21 : 23-25.) How did Jesus improve upon this? (Matthew 5 : 38-42.) Read Jesus' law of love. (Matthew 5 : 43-48.)

For You to Think About

Do you know of any jealousy among the leaders in your town? Why is this so? What might help overcome it? Do you know of any members of your class at school who are jealous of one another? Why? How might they become friendly? What are some of the things that break up the good spirit of a class? How can each person help build a happy class?

CHAPTER IX

ONE DAY BY THE LAKE

W E have now noted different things about Jesus'
life in Galilee — his teachings, his cures of the
sick, his friends and his foes. Let us, in this chapter,
try to understand how life went on for Jesus from day
to day. It may be well to say just here that the stories
regarding him which have been saved do not tell us
with any sort of exactness how long he lived as a
teacher. We know he was about thirty when he began,
and there is some reason to think he carried on his
work for about three years. Most of that time his home
was at Capernaum, and he took short trips among the
towns and villages of Galilee. It is quite possible,
however, that he did not have so long a time to teach
as three years. It may have been less than two. But
in any event he spent the greater part of the time in
the country near the lake.

At first his efforts met with great success. Large
numbers of people gathered about him wherever he
went. Poor crazy men and women were made well in
mind; others who had blindness or leprosy or fevers
were made well in body. The story of his blessed
power was carried to every town and village. Along
the roadsides people waited for him to pass that they
might see him. One day some women brought him
their little children that he might touch them and so
bless them. In those days children were not treated so

kindly as they are now. Even the young men who
made up his group of twelve tried to stop the mothers
in what they were doing. On that day Jesus made the
answer that we always love to remember:

"Let the little children come unto me and forbid
them not." And then the story says, ... "he took them
up in his arms and blessed them."

Sometimes, again, the plan he had made was suddenly changed by someone's coming to him in great
trouble to ask his aid. One day he had been across the
Lake of Galilee to the eastern shore. Probably it was
not for long; perhaps for only one night. But when
his little boat again touched the shore near Capernaum, he found a large number of people waiting for
him. They wanted to hear him speak. They never
knew what wonderful thing he might do. Hardly,
however, had be begun to speak with them when a man
who had charge of the synagogue, or the church, as
we call it, pushed his way through the crowd and
asked Jesus to listen to him.

"My little girl," he said, "is so sick that I fear she
may die. No one has been able to help her. Won't you
come and see if you can do anything for her?"

Jesus could not refuse this appeal. With a large
number of people following him he set out at once on
the short walk to the house where the little girl lay
sick. On the way there he felt someone give a pull
upon his long outer robe. Every man then as now in
the land of Palestine wore what we might call a loose

cloak with loose sleeves. It was easy to reach out and take hold of this as a person walked past one.

Jesus stopped. "Who touched my clothes?" he asked. One of his band of twelve spoke up at once and said in surprise, "A good many people must have touched you." The streets were narrow. The crowd filled them. Eager to keep close to Jesus and to see and hear all that might take place, the people pressed close up to him, so that, as the young man said, many persons may have touched him. But Jesus knew that the pull on his robe was not due just to the pushing of the eager people. He looked carefully around on those near enough to have touched him. Almost immediately his eye fell upon a woman, pale and clearly ill. As he looked at her, she came a step nearer.

"It was I, Master," she said.

She did not know what Jesus would say, but she felt that he had discovered at once what she had done. Perhaps she had done wrong, but she could only trust he would not be angry.

"I have been sick for many years," she said to Jesus. "Nearly all the money I had has been spent. None of the doctors has cured me. I heard of you. I thought that if I could only touch you, I might get well."

Very kindly Jesus spoke to her: "I will help you. You may go home sure that you are cured." All this had taken but a few minutes. It was just as Jesus had finished speaking and was about to walk on again that someone else pushed through the crowd.

"It is no use," he broke out. "The little girl is dead."

The father, who all the time had kept by Jesus' side, anxious to guide and hurry him on the way to the house, was in despair. But Jesus comforted him quietly.

"Do not give up hope," he said.

In a few moments he reached the house. At the door he asked all the people to wait. Even of his band of twelve only three went into the house with him. He found the little girl lying so quiet that she seemed, indeed, to be dead. Jesus walked up to the bed, first asking the people in the house who were crying and sobbing to quiet their sorrow. Then he took the small hand that lay so white and cold on the sheet.

"My little girl," he said, "you can get up."

And to the surprise of everyone the child did so.

QUESTIONS AND TOPICS FOR STUDY

About how old was Jesus when he began to teach? How long is he supposed to have taught? Where did he spend the greater part of this time? Tell of his early success.

How did Jesus feel toward children? How was he different in this from most of the others of his day? What did Jesus say about the children? What did he do?

Where did Jesus go one day? What happened when he returned? Whose little girl was ill? Why would Jesus especially wish to help in this case?

What happened on the way to her house? What kind of outer garment do the people of Palestine wear? Why were the twelve surprised that Jesus should notice that somebody had touched him? Why had he noticed it? Who had touched Jesus? What was the matter with the woman? What did Jesus say to her?

Who then pushed through the crowd? What did he say? How did the father feel? What did Jesus say to him? What did they find at the house? What did Jesus do? Can you imagine what the parents of the little girl thought and how they felt? (Describe this in your diary story.)

Further Discoveries

How did people cure the sick in those days? (Mark 5:23; 6:5.) What did Jesus think was necessary if one was to be helped? (Mark 5:34, 36.) What took place in an oriental house as soon as anyone was thought to have died? (Matthew 9:23; Mark 5:38.) What did Jesus seem to think about this? (Mark 5:39, 40.) Was Jesus anxious for people to know what he could do? (Mark 5:43; Matthew 8:4.)

CHAPTER X

A Day at Nazareth

ONE day Jesus set out from Capernaum and walked over the hills to Nazareth. It was a journey which might have taken two days if he did not tarry long anywhere. He may have stopped at some little village over night, or perhaps he lay down to sleep on the hillslopes under the stars. His young men were not with him on this journey. Jesus was glad to be in his own town again. Stories of what he had done had reached Nazareth, and the people were a good deal excited over them. They had long known Jesus as a young man and a good workman who built houses and repaired them. It seemed quite impossible to think of him as a great teacher and a wonderful healer of the sick. They were at once curious and doubtful.

There was a custom in those days for the minister to ask any guest to read the Bible in the church service. On the last day of his visit, which was the Sabbath, Jesus was invited to do this. He read a part of the writing of the prophet Isaiah. If you would like to know just what he read, turn to that book in your Bible and read the first verses of the sixty-first chapter. Books in those days were in the form of rolls of writing. When he had finished the reading, Jesus handed the roll to the man whose duty it was to see that it was safely put away, and sat down near the pulpit. Then,

45

as was his right, he began to speak about what he had
read:

"You wanted to see me do wonderful things here in
this town where you all know me. I cannot do them
except where people believe in me. Where they do
that my words seem true and my deeds great. If you
do not think I am able to do the things the prophet
wrote about, you will be disappointed in me."

His words made the people very angry. You see
they thought he was just the village carpenter and
there was no reason to have respect for what he said.
When he seemed to make himself out more important
than the rest of the people, they were so angry that
they wanted to hurt him. They broke up the service
and pushed and pulled him roughly through the
streets.

Nazareth was built upon hills rising steeply from
the plain. Beyond the houses of the town you come out
upon bare jagged rocks. There are high peaks and
deep gullies. One needs to walk carefully to avoid a
fall. A man thrown about roughly might easily be
injured or even killed. Jesus' peril was great. Everyone who might have been his friend was his enemy
that day. But Jesus all alone was more than a match
for the crowd. We may be sure he did not strike any
one of them. To do this would have invited their
blows and he might have been killed then and there.
Instead he spoke quietly to them. They saw he was
not afraid. What he said we do not know, but we

do know that the angry, excited mob of people was brought to reason. Seeing him so cool and brave they felt a sort of awe. Then and there they began to wonder if he was indeed a greater one than they had supposed. Steadily he looked first at one, then at another. Those who were holding him loosened their rough grasp. Slowly the crowd slipped back from him. And with that splendid courage in his look and strong calm in his manner which they had failed to break, but which had broken their purpose, he walked out of the town, out into the hills, to begin his journey back to Capernaum.

Of course, every day was neither so exciting as this nor so full of happenings as was that other day when he healed the little girl who was thought to be dead. Some days he spent in talking quietly with friends or in walking to a town where perhaps lived some man who had heard him at Capernaum or had been healed of disease by Jesus, and who wished Jesus to speak there and become known. Palestine is not a large country, but to visit its towns and villages, walking on foot and spending even a day or so in each place, would take a long time. However, we are coming near to the end of the story of these days, and we must see what things happened to bring that end about.

QUESTIONS AND TOPICS FOR STUDY

Where did Jesus go from Capernaum one day? How long a journey was this? Did anyone go with him? Why might Jesus be glad to be back in Nazareth? What did the people there think of him? Why was it hard for them to think of him as a great teacher?

Where did Jesus go on the Sabbath? What did he do there? What did the people of his own town think when they heard him speak? What did they expect to see him do? Why were they disappointed? What did they threaten to do to Jesus? How did he escape?

Where did Jesus go next? How long would it have taken to visit all the towns of Palestine? Tell how some of Jesus' days may have been spent.

Further Discoveries

Did Jesus usually go to the synagogue, or as we should say, to church? (Luke 4: 16.) Compare the words Jesus spoke on this occasion with those of the prophet Isaiah. (Luke 4: 16-27, and Isaiah 61 : 1-3.) How did he carry out these words in what he did? What report was sent to John about Jesus' work? (Matthew 11 : 2-5.) What did the people think when they heard Jesus speak in the synagogue? (Luke 4: 22, and Matthew 13: 54.) Why were they surprised? (Matthew 13: 55, 56.) Did he know they expected him to do something wonderful? (Luke 4: 23.) Why didn't he? (Matthew 13: 57, 58.)

Something to Do

Report in your diary about this visit to Jesus' home town.

CHAPTER XI

A LITTLE BOY AND MANY PEOPLE

YOU will remember that there were certain people in the land who did not like Jesus and who wanted to stop his teaching. As the days went by their feeling against Jesus grew stronger. What finally led to an open break between them and him was their fear that, if they did not stop him at once, he might become too popular to be controlled. One day something happened that caused a great change in the way Jesus had been living.

Shortly before this, Jesus had sent out his young men, two by two, to go to places he had not been able to visit himself. They had been gone for a few weeks, telling here and there what Jesus had taught them. Very many interesting things had happened, and they were anxious to talk them over with him. On the day when the last of them returned to Capernaum, Jesus suggested that they go away together to a quiet place in the hills where they could be by themselves. They decided to sail along the shore and find such a spot. It was easy to get a boat. It may have been, indeed, the very one Peter and Andrew had used. They all embarked expecting a restful time alone with Jesus. But it was going to be a different day from what they had expected.

The sailing away of the boat was noticed. There were many people who wished to talk with him. It was thought that he would not go so very far. By hastening on foot along the shore, they could meet the boat as it drew in to the land. So Jesus and his young men found a large number of people waiting for them as they finally dropped their sail and pulled their boat up on the pebbly beach. Jesus could not refuse to speak with them. Going back a little from the shore to a spot where there was some shade from the sun, for it is very hot at midday by the lake, they sat down on the grass. For a long time he talked with them. One thing led to another. The hours slipped by. Finally as there came a pause in the questions and his answers, one of his young men stepped up to him and said: "Master, have you thought that evening is coming on and these people have had nothing to eat? It is not possible to bring any food out to them. Ought we not to get them started home at once?"

Jesus knew that it was a long walk home. He also thought that some of the people, at least, must have brought some food. So he told his young men to find out about this and to have the people make up into groups of families and neighbors. Soon the word was brought to Jesus that this had been done. He was also told that there was one little boy who had some bread and fish which his mother had given him for a picnic lunch. Jesus asked the little boy if he would share this with others. Very gladly he offered to do this, proud that he could be of some help in Jesus' plans for the people.

Then Jesus stood before the crowd, and taking the bread and the fish in his hands told them how the little boy had brought the lunch there to eat himself, but finding that some people had nothing he was generously offering to share it with others. How fine it would be, he said, if everyone who had any food would do likewise! And now something wonderful happened. When people are hungry and there is not much food, everyone who has any usually wants to keep it all for himself. But Jesus had made these people see how fine it was to be generous, kind, and thoughtful of others. The result was that, instead of thinking first of saving what he had, everyone was eager to share what he had with his neighbors.

As Jesus knew would be the case there was plenty of food if all who had any shared with all who needed. So, although there seemed at first to be only the two little loaves of bread and a few dried fish, there was food left over after all had eaten. But it seemed a remarkable thing, and it was so indeed. To make a whole crowd kind and generous is something so great that it is no wonder the story of it was told far and wide, until after a while it came to be said that Jesus made the little boy's lunch feed five thousand people. That, indeed, is what he did; only not by a trick of magic, but by his power over people's lives.

A very important result was that the people became very enthusiastic for Jesus. Everyone was speaking about him. And so many were speaking in his praise that those who did not like him felt they must act quickly and strongly to drive him away. So it happened that they went where he went, criticised what he said, stirred up others to find fault with him and made it plain that more and more his daily work would be one of dispute and trouble. At last Jesus felt that things could not go on in that way; and he decided to leave for a time, at least, the country near the lake he loved so well.

QUESTIONS AND TOPICS FOR STUDY

Why did certain people wish to stop Jesus from teaching? Why did Jesus go off to the hills with his friends one day? How did they reach the spot? Why were they followed? How did the people get to the place where Jesus was? Why did Jesus speak to them? How long did he stay with them? What did one of the young men finally suggest? Did Jesus do this? Why not? What did he tell his helpers to do? What did one little boy have? Why do you think he was glad to share? What did Jesus do with this little lunch? What effect might that have had on the others? What made other people willing to share?

Do you think Jesus may have said something to them that day that made them wish to be kind and generous? What do you think he may have told them? What happened when all began to share? Do you think this was remarkable? Why?

What would you have done with your lunch if you had been there? How many people were probably fed because of the lad's sharing? Was there any trick about this? Why was it Jesus was able to accomplish so remarkable a thing? How much power does it take to change people's hearts? Why did Jesus possess that kind of power?

What was the result of this event? What kind of people liked Jesus better than ever? Which ones disliked him even more? What did they try to do? What did Jesus do for a while?

Further Discoveries

How much impression do you think this incident made on the people? (John 6: 14, 15.) Why would the people consider Jesus a prophet? Why would they wish to make him king? Why did Jesus not want to be their king? What was his work to be? How popular do you think this story of the feeding of the multitude might become? How many of the Gospels tell about it? (Read Matthew 14: 13-21; Mark 6: 30-44; Luke 9: 10-17; John 6: 1-15.) Which Gospel tells twice about feeding a multitude? (See also Matthew 15: 29-39.) Which Gospel tells the story of the boy with his lunch? What feast was near? (John 6: 4.) What kind of bread would the people have at that time? (Exodus 12: 14, 15.)

Something to Do

Continue your diary. How can you describe the multitude following Jesus? Who will be especially eager to hear what he has to say? How will you bring out the contrast between Jesus' attitude toward the people and that of the disciples? How exciting will you make it when Jesus tells the people to sit down in companies, as if something were about to happen? Will you be curious to know what good the little boy's lunch can do? How will you describe the passing out of the food? What will you say about the enthusiasm of the people for Jesus after this? What about his enemies? What will you have Jesus do when they try to make him king?

CHAPTER XII

A Brave Resolve

IF you will look at a map of the United States you will see that for anyone who lives in the northern part of our country it is not far to the line between Canada and the United States. Across that line one is in another country with a different government, different laws, and some different customs. Just so, by walking north for a few hours from the region about the lake, Jesus would come into another country where his enemies had no power and where he would not be well known. For a little while, we do not know how long, he and his young men stayed in this country. It is overshadowed by great mountains and, like Palestine to the south, it is bordered by the Mediterranean Sea.

While there Jesus cured the daughter of a woman who somehow had heard of what he had done in Galilee and believed he would help her also. But he did no public teaching, giving all his time to his twelve young men. One day they made him very happy by telling him how much they loved and honored him. One of them, Peter, the story of whose call to give up fishing and follow Jesus you will remember, told him that they felt he was the great leader for whom everyone had been watching and praying. The day this happened was a memorable day indeed for Jesus.

But it was not wise or desirable that they should go

on living for a long time in this northern country.
They could not do much good there just then. The
great question was what to do next. An event that was
soon to occur at Jerusalem finally seems to have decided Jesus' plans. This event was the Feast of the
Passover. You recall the story of how the Hebrew
people, long centuries before this, had been slaves in
Egypt; how at last a great leader, Moses, led them out
of bondage; and how every year thereafter they had a
religious and patriotic ceremony or service to honor
the memory of this event.

When the Passover time came, people from all over
Palestine who could make the trip journeyed up to
Jerusalem and stayed there for several days, until on
the last day of the festival the Passover supper was
served to everyone in family or friendly groups, as
American people eat their Thanksgiving dinner.
There were thousands and thousands of visitors in
Jerusalem at this time. It was the time and place of
all others when one could be seen and heard by the
most people.

Jesus decided to go to Jerusalem for this Passover.
It was a dangerous thing to do. The Pharisees who
disliked what he had done in Galilee were sure to be
against his plans at this great national gathering. And
at Jerusalem there were much more dreaded enemies
to be met, a group of people called Sadducees. These
people, holding offices in the temple and in the city
government, were certain to think that Jesus was mak-

ing trouble. They would fear lest in stirring up dis-
order he would interfere with their plans. Perhaps,
indeed, they would be blamed for all he did. Then
they might have their offices taken from them. This
would all be very disagreeable and they were determined to prevent it. Thus Jesus found them his cruel
foes, ready to kill him if necessary.

And yet he decided to go to Jerusalem where all
this danger lay. Why did he do so? There were two
reasons that we may name. He felt that in Jerusalem
at the Passover would be the best possible chance to
reach the people with his teaching. If they would
listen and find the better way of life which he could
point out, then and there, if ever, would be the time
and place to set forth the truth. In the second place,
Jesus had been growing to feel that even if he was put
to death, his dying would draw people's attention to
him, so that his death would really help, not prevent,
what he wanted to do.

What a brave resolve that was of Jesus! To go on,
though he were to be killed; to teach at the cost of his
life! Yet to this Jesus set his steps, willing to die if
that were the result, and hopeful that his dying would
do even more than his living. So we must follow him
on the journey south to Jerusalem and then for a little
less than a week longer in that great city — the most
important week anyone has ever lived on earth.

QUESTIONS AND TOPICS FOR STUDY

To what sort of country did Jesus go next? What did he do while there? What did Peter tell him one day? How did Jesus feel when he heard this? Why was it not the best thing for them to stay in the northern country?

What event was soon to take place at Jerusalem? What was the meaning of this feast? From how far away did people travel to Jerusalem at this time? Do you remember when Jesus first went to Jerusalem for this feast? What happened at that time? Do you suppose some of those who heard him at the temple would recognize him again if they saw him? What might they think of him now?

How many people would be in Jerusalem? Why was it especially dangerous for Jesus to go this time? What two groups of people would be hostile? Did Jesus realize the danger? Why then did he decide to go? Do you think his decision was wise or foolish? Why?

Further Discoveries

What did some of the people think about Jesus? (Matthew 16: 13, 14.) Why should they think he was an ancient prophet come back to life? Did the people of those days think prophets could be brought back to life? Read an old story about the prophet Samuel. (1 Samuel 28: 3-15.) Did people believe a prophet had the power to bring others back to life? (Read about the prophet Elisha, in 2 Kings 4: 32-37, and 13: 20, 21.) What two great prophets were said to have appeared talking to Jesus? (Matthew 17: 1-8.) Who thought that Jesus was John the Baptizer come back to life? (Mark 6: 14-16.) Why should he have thought so?

CHAPTER XIII

A Long Journey

NOW will you look again at a map of the land where Jesus lived? You will see the part marked Galilee in which were Nazareth and Capernaum and the Lake of Galilee. Almost all our story has so far been about this part of Palestine. South of Galilee you see the part marked Samaria. When David was king this was just as much a part of his kingdom as Massachusetts is a part of the United States. In the days of David's grandson, however, the kingdom was divided into two unequal parts. In Samaria was a rival capital to Jerusalem. Nevertheless the people of Samaria were of just the same race and blood as those who still held Jerusalem as their chief city. But after many years this northern kingdom was conquered by a foreign enemy and the citizens scattered. Finally in their place grew up some people called Samaritans, who disliked and were disliked by the Jews living south of them.

Below Samaria on the map you see Judea, smaller than Galilee or Samaria. It is a mountainous bit of land and not so good for farming. But in Judea is Jerusalem. Here as nowhere else lived the memories of the past and the hopes for days to come. In Jerusalem were kept all the great festivals of patriotism and religion and especially the Passover, to which we are about to follow Jesus.

It is well to be clear about these things because they
explain the way Jesus traveled to the feast. The easy,
simple thing was to walk due south from Galilee
through the midst of Samaria. But when he sent two
of his young men ahead to arrange for places to stop,
the Samaritan people said they did not want Jesus or
any other Jews of Galilee to go through their country.
Rather than have any trouble, Jesus chose another way.
He followed the Jordan River, crossing over to its
eastern bank and going south through a country called
Perea.

It was not a very long journey. If Jesus had been
inclined to hurry he could have arrived in Jerusalem
within a week. But Jesus seems to have gone slowly,
stopping often on the way and spending such time as
seemed worth while at one town after another. He
found the people interested to hear him. They brought
to him questions to be answered. Sometimes they told
him their troubles and asked Jesus what to do. Fre-
quently Jesus replied with a story which made things
very clear.

Some of the most beautiful and interesting of all
his stories, or parables, seem to have been told during
this journey. There is the story of the boy who asked
his father to give him right away the money which
might become his when, after his father's death, the
property was divided. With this money he left home
and spent it so foolishly that soon he did not have any
left. He was so poor that he had to take the meanest,

most disagreeable sort of job, the caring for a herd of
pigs. How sorry he was for the way he had wasted his
money! How he wished he were once more at home!
Then one day he said to himself: "I am going home.
I do not know that they will let me stay. I have been
so bad and foolish I do not deserve to stay. But I must
see my father again."

So he started. His father had never for a moment
forgotten him. The story of his bad and silly actions
had been carried to his home, but his father kept on
hoping that at last he would see how foolish he was.
Often this father of his looked down the road that led
into the far country, wondering if the boy would come
back. Then there came the day when the boy returning by that road caught sight of his father's house.
He walked toward it, not knowing what to expect but
ready to tell his father how very sorry he was and to
ask for a chance to live and work at home as of old.

Almost at the same moment his father saw him. He
did not wait for the young man to reach the house but
went out to meet him. There on the roadway the boy
learned that his father forgave him, and that since he
was truly sorry he was to have another chance. "God,"
said Jesus, "is like that father. And we who are like
that foolish boy are not hated because we do bad
things but are waited for until we are sorry; and we
are loved always."

Jesus told other stories, which you will find in the
Book of Luke in the New Testament, in the chapters

from the eleventh to the eighteenth. Almost all that is told us there is thought to have happened on that journey through the land of Perea to Jerusalem.

QUESTIONS AND TOPICS FOR STUDY

Find these places on your map:

1. Galilee. Find two cities connected with Jesus,—Nazareth and Capernaum. Point out the Lake of Galilee.
2. Samaria. Find also the city of Samaria.
3. Judea. What is the name of its capital? Locate it.
4. Find Perea. Point out Jericho and Bethany. Trace the journey Jesus may have taken to reach Jerusalem, if he started at Capernaum and went through Perea, Jericho, and Bethany.

What do you remember about Galilee and its two cities you found? What can you tell of the history of Samaria? Why did the Jews and the Samaritans dislike each other? What kind of country is most of Judea? What took place at Jerusalem? How would Jesus go to Jerusalem from Galilee if he wished to take the shortest way? Why did he not do this? How did he go finally? How long would that way take? Why did it take Jesus longer than usual? What stories did he tell the people at this time?

Further Discoveries

Find a story about a rich man. (Luke 12:16-21.) Find one about a king who prepared a feast. (Luke 14:16-24.) Read about a lost sheep. (Luke 15:3-7.) Find a story of a piece of lost silver. (Luke 15:8-10.) Read the story of a loving father. (Luke 15:11-32.) Now read about the faithful servants. (Luke 19:12-26.)

Something to Do

Besides continuing your diary, outline as you would play it the story of the loving father, or of the faithful servants. Write out the speeches of the different characters.

CHAPTER XIV

In Jericho and Bethany

IN the hot depths of the Jordan valley is a very, very old city, called Jericho. Jesus and his young men reached there one day in their journey towards Jerusalem. In those days it was a busy place. The story of his deeds and words had gone on before him and a big crowd gathered to see him. Two things happened there which were remembered ever after. One was the giving of sight to a blind man. Palestine had, and still has today, many people whose eyes are hurt by the strong sun and by lack of care. Just as Jesus helped people sick with other diseases, he helped those who had lost their sight.

The other interesting thing happened in this way. There was a man in the city whose name was Zaccheus. His business was collecting the money which people had to pay to the Roman Government. We pay taxes in this way to our government, and we know that it is right and proper for the money to be collected. It is spent on our schools and roads and police and other things we all need in our life together. The trouble in Palestine was that the money was paid over not to their own officers but to this foreign country of Rome, whose soldiers had conquered Palestine. The people felt that much of it was not spent for their good but for the Romans themselves. So they hated the men

that collected the money, and Zaccheus was one of
these men.

He was a short man. The crowd in the road was
large and he could not catch sight of Jesus. But he
was determined that he would see him. With this in
mind he climbed up into a tree, and when Jesus came
by there he was. Jesus felt that any man who would
do that must be interested in him. He stopped and told
Zaccheus that he would go to his house if Zaccheus
would like to have him. Zaccheus had not been a good
man. He had taken more money for the taxes than he
should have, and since people hated him, he had returned their hate. But now when Jesus spoke and
acted with such kindness, Zaccheus felt that he must
be a decent, good man. He said to Jesus, "Just so far
as I can I will give back any money I have taken
wrongly, and I will use my other money so as to do all
the good I can."

This story shows us how Jesus made people feel
when they really tried to understand him. Zaccheus
was only one of many who, from living in a bad or
foolish way, turned to be good and brave and clean in
their deeds. Jesus made people want to do right and
showed them how they could.

After this little visit with Zaccheus, Jesus started
again on the way to Jerusalem. Jericho is in a deep
valley. Jerusalem is on the top of a mountain. So
this final part of Jesus' journey is a steep rocky road
through wild desolate country, that very country, in-

deed, where John had lived and where Jesus had gone
in the first days after he had decided to become a
teacher about God. There is an interesting story Jesus
told once about a man who was almost killed by robbers on this very road. You can read it in the tenth
chapter of the Gospel of Luke.

No robbers, however, attacked Jesus on his way.
He finally came to a little village about six miles away
from Jerusalem, high up on the mountainside. From
its streets one can look back over the long ascent and
see the Dead Sea near Jericho, far below. It was a
quiet place to rest, and a safe place to stay. Jesus had
some good friends there who were anxious to have him
as a guest. In every way it seemed best to make his
home there during the Passover.

Each morning he could walk into Jerusalem and
spend the day there. Each evening he could return to
Bethany, feeling sure that his enemies would not trouble him there among his friends. It was Friday when
he reached Bethany. Saturday in Palestine was the day
people ceased work and play and went to church. And
so we think of Jesus on the last day of the week, called
the Sabbath, in that little village on the mountainside.

QUESTIONS AND TOPICS FOR STUDY

Why was there a crowd at Jericho waiting for Jesus? Why
are there many blind people in Palestine? What was Jesus able
to do for one blind man at Jericho?

Who was Zaccheus? What are taxes usually spent for? Who
received the tax money in Palestine? Why did the people dislike

paying taxes to the Romans? Why did they feel that tax collectors were their enemies? Why do you suppose Zaccheus wanted to see Jesus? What did he do in order to see Jesus? What did Jesus say to him? Why? What mistakes had Zaccheus made before this? Why did he feel he must be different now? What promise did he make? Why do you think Jesus made people feel like this?

What is the country like from Jericho to Jerusalem? Read a story Jesus told about something that happened there. (Luke 10: 25-37.) What do you think of that kind of neighborliness? Was Jesus that kind of neighbor?

Where did Jesus stay during the Passover? What can be seen from Bethany? (Look it up on your map. Find how near Jerusalem is, and where the Dead Sea lies.) Why did Jesus stay in Bethany? Where did he plan to go each morning? On what day of the week did he reach Bethany?

Something to Do

Add to your dramatized stories that of the Good Samaritan.

CHAPTER XV

THE ARRIVAL IN JERUSALEM

THE sun rose over the mountains of Moab, far to the east, bringing in the first day of the week, and Jesus made ready to go to Jerusalem. Accompanied by his young men he left Bethany and walked up the slope of the mountain beyond which lay the city. Nowadays, the road circles the slope somewhat below the summit. In those days the path went straight over the top, as it is not too steep for travelers on foot. But Jesus did not plan to go in that way all the distance.

Many long years before this, one of the great men of his nation had written a poem speaking of a king who should come to them " riding upon an ass." (Ass is the name for the small donkeys that are used for much of the hard work of carrying loads in Palestine.) What this writer wanted to make clear was that the true king would not come as would a soldier on a war-horse to conquer by force, but rather to win his place in a peaceful way. Jesus felt that he was truly the one who could help the people as no one ever had done before. He believed that thus he could rightly claim to be the one who had been promised as the true leader. But he was most anxious that the people should not think of him as a general to raise armies, or as a king, spending great sums of money and ordering people to do his will.

In order, then, to come to them in just the way that

should make plain what he wanted to do for them, he decided to enter Jerusalem as the writer of old had described. With this in mind he had made an arrangement with a man who had one of the donkeys about which I told you. Now as Jesus with his young men came near to a little cluster of houses through which the path ran, he told two of them to hurry on ahead.

"You will find," he said, "a colt tied near one of the houses. It has been put there for me. Unloose it and return at once. If anybody asks you why you are doing this, just say that the Master has need of it. Then it will be understood that you come from me, and no other question will be asked."

The two young men did as Jesus told them, and when someone wanted to know why they were leading away the animal, the answer Jesus had told them to give explained everything satisfactorily. When they got back to Jesus and the others, they put one of their long outer garments on the donkey's back for a saddle. Jesus mounted and set forth in this way for the rest of the way to Jerusalem.

Meanwhile the news had gone ahead that Jesus was riding thither. There had come to Jerusalem as pilgrims to the Passover a considerable number of people from Galilee who had known Jesus, had heard him, had perhaps come to believe in him. At any rate he was a man of their own part of the country. Among the proud Jews of Jerusalem who thought themselves better than the Galilean people, the latter were glad of the chance to show that they, too, had famous men. They were ready to hail Jesus as one for their own sakes, although they might not have been loyal to him at home.

These Galileans had probably been camping out upon the mountainside, because Jerusalem could not house all the pilgrims and because it was cheaper to live in the open air. As Jesus' little party came on towards the city the pilgrims saw him. Immediately they began to shout. Today people would cry out "Hurrah." These Galileans called out "Hosanna, Hosanna." The shouting of the first to see and greet him attracted others. In a short time there was a considerable crowd following him and surrounding him. They broke off branches of the palm trees and waved them like flags. They took off their outer garments and spread them in the path along which he rode, and their shouts rang out in the clear morning air.

So Jesus reached the summit of the Mount of Olives and began the long descent into the valley. From the top there is one of the most beautiful views in all the world. Eastward and northward and southward there are mountains and open country. But directly westward on two rocky hills, across the deep ravine into which the mountainside runs down, is the city of Jerusalem surrounded by its walls, gleaming with white and gold. One sees the whole of it at once, brilliant in the mountain air and bright sunlight. You can imagine some of the feelings it stirred in Jesus,—

the beauty of it all, the sense of the city's great past, his wonder whether it would listen to him or turn away. It would have been natural for him to have felt the danger that might be waiting there. But he did not think of going back. Instead he rode quietly but bravely forward, down the long mountain slope, through the ravine, up the shorter ascent beyond, and so through the gates into the city.

QUESTIONS AND TOPICS FOR STUDY

How did Jesus plan to go to Jerusalem? Find the writing from the Old Testament which Jesus probably had in mind when he chose to ride upon an animal of peace (Zechariah 9: 9.) What did kings choose to ride upon? Do you know what warriors often rode in, when going to battle? (Zechariah 9: 10.) Why do you think Jesus chose an animal of peace? What kind of king did he wish to be?

What had he been teaching the people all this while about living together? How had he practiced this teaching in the case of Zaccheus?

Who saw him riding into Jerusalem? Where had they probably been camping? What did they call out when they saw Jesus? What did they wave as he approached? What did they spread before him in the way? Why? Do you think they would have liked to see him become king? Read again what happened when the multitude was fed. (John 6: 14, 15.) Do you think Jesus wished to be thought of as this kind of king? Why not? What did he say about his kingdom? (John 18: 36.)

Further Discoveries

Describe what Jesus would have seen from the top of the Mount of Olives. What might he have been thinking as he saw Jerusalem before him? Read what he once said about the city. (Luke 13: 34, 35.) Compare the last verse with the greeting of the multitude as he rode into Jerusalem in triumph. (Luke 19: 37, 38.) Read another lament over the city. (Luke 19: 41-44.)

CHAPTER XVI

THE DAYS THAT FOLLOWED

SO JESUS came to Jerusalem. It is impossible to tell accurately just what he did each of the first four days of the week. We have the story of certain things that happened between the Sunday morning and Thursday evening. We know, too, that every evening until Thursday Jesus walked back to Bethany and spent the night there. He did this because after a busy day among the crowds he could find more rest in the little village than in Jerusalem. But he also did it because, as he soon discovered, there was great danger to him in Jerusalem.

When the groups of people who disliked and feared Jesus saw the enthusiasm shown for him, they decided that they must do all they could to prevent him from gaining followers. Very quickly their resolve was made to put him to death. They were led to decide this with the more energy because, after reaching the city, Jesus said certain things reproving them for the way they lived, and for their treatment of others less fortunate than they. Knowing that the people in the city were either friendly to Jesus or at least not ready to do him any harm, they did not see at first just how they could get Jesus into their power without the possibility of a riot. If they tried to make Jesus a prisoner in Jerusalem, and if he called for help and received it, and if all this meant a great disturbance, they knew that the Roman officer who ruled the city might punish them for causing the trouble. Instead of harming Jesus they would only hurt themselves. The question was how to catch him when no help was near.

It was just then that they received aid from one of Jesus' young men, whose name was Judas. He became a traitor to Jesus. Going to the enemies of Jesus he said that if they would pay him some money, he would let them know when Jesus could be made a prisoner. Why did Judas do this? He never left any statement to explain his action. After Jesus was put to death he felt so sorry for what he had done that he took his own life. We have to try to imagine what led him to the horrible deed.

Probably he had joined Jesus expecting him to be a leader whose deeds would bring money or glory to his followers. Then when Jesus showed that no such rewards were coming, Judas felt disappointed. As the time went by and people turned away from Jesus, Judas grew bitter in his disappointment. At last, seeing how in Jerusalem the richest, most powerful people were Jesus' enemies, he let himself believe that Jesus was mistaken in what he was trying to do. It would be well, so he may have said to himself, to have Jesus stopped from teaching. Judas may never have thought Jesus would be killed. But when he became a traitor to his leader and friend, he was in part to blame for all that happened later.

Meanwhile, during those first four days of the week

Jesus was coming to Jerusalem in the morning and speaking to various groups in the temple courts. It became clear to him right away that, although the Galilean people had given him a splendid welcome, they were not able to influence the city to accept his teaching. Instead of finding friendly listeners eager to learn what he might teach, Jesus met all sorts of people clearly bent on confusing or outwitting him. They tried to engage him in disputes where they could show him forth in a bad light. Jesus always escaped their plots by his answers; but he could not change the minds or hearts of these enemies who, when defeated in words, became the more anxious to turn to force.

Even then he might have escaped, but he would not give up his work of teaching. He felt he ought to go on trying to help people understand God and treat one another kindly. So with great courage and patience and energy he did what he could among the crowds in Jerusalem by day, and each evening turned his steps to Bethany, where he was sure of a friendly greeting and safe in a friendly home.

QUESTIONS AND TOPICS FOR STUDY

Where did Jesus go each evening? Why? What were his enemies planning to do? Why did they dislike Jesus? Why could they not take him at once? Who decided to help capture Jesus? Why may he have done this?

What was Jesus doing during the first four days of the week? Why were the Galilean people of so little help in his work? Why did some of the people try to engage Jesus in disputes? Could Jesus win in these disputes? How? Could he change the hearts of the arguers? Why not? How do you suppose a man felt after he had been defeated in argument before a crowd of people?

How might Jesus have escaped danger? Why didn't he?

Further Discoveries

What did Jesus do when he went into the temple at Jerusalem? (Luke 19: 45, 46.) Where did Jesus go most often? Why? (Luke 19: 47, 48.) What did Jesus reply when asked his authority for what he said and did? (Luke 20: 1-8.) Where do you think John got his inspiration to preach and baptize? Where do you think Jesus' authority was from? Read a story Jesus told at this time, and see if you can discover its meaning. (Luke 20: 9-19.) What did Jesus say about paying tribute money to Cæsar? (Luke 20: 20-26.) What did he say about the scribes? (Luke 20: 45-47.) What did he say about a widow's offering? (Luke 21: 1-4.)

Something to Do

Add to your diary what happened when Jesus went into the temple each day to teach the people.

CHAPTER XVII

THURSDAY EVENING

IT WAS Thursday, the day when in the evening the people would gather in their family groups — or, if they were alone in the city, with other friends — and eat the Passover meal. Jesus planned to keep this custom in the company of his young men. He had arranged in advance to have a room ready. That Thursday morning he did not go into Jerusalem. Until then, his young men knew only that Jesus and they would keep the Passover feast somewhere together. That morning they asked him what plans he had made.

In reply Jesus told two of them to be ready to go into Jerusalem ahead of all the rest. At a certain place they would meet a man waiting for them to come. This man would carry a water jar.

"Follow him," Jesus told them, "and he will take you to a certain house. Tell the owner of that house that you want to know about the room which the Teacher is to have for the Passover. He will show you a large room all ready for us. Make ready the meal there."

We have seen how calmly and bravely Jesus went on his way, despite all opposition shown him and all danger threatened. He did not intend, however, to be foolish. He knew that the bitter enemies in Jerusalem waited only the chance to make him prisoner, and that if they could only come upon him when he was alone with his young men, as he would be when eating the Passover supper, they could carry out their purpose. So he guarded against their knowing where he would be. He had made his plans secretly and carefully. Not until the two men sent on ahead had followed the man with the water jar and so reached the house, did any of Jesus' closest friends know the place.

There was yet a further danger to be met. It was part of the Passover custom for the Jews to remain the rest of the night in Jerusalem. So Jesus had planned that when they left the room they should go together to a quiet place on the side of the mountain, a kind of garden or grove of olive trees. This was so near to Jerusalem that they would still be true to the custom of the Passover, but it was not a place that his enemies would think of searching. All would indeed have gone well but for one fact, the traitor in that little band which Jesus thought to be altogether loyal.

In the afternoon, with Peter and John and all the rest including Judas, Jesus set out from Bethany for Jerusalem. At once they made their way to the house where the Passover was ready. The two who had gone ahead had found everything as Jesus had planned and were awaiting him there. As the darkness fell over the city they all gathered about the table, and the ceremony of the Passover meal was begun.

Jesus, at least, felt it to be an unusually solemn hour. He knew that at any moment his enemies might be

upon him in spite of all his vigilance. He had done
everything he could to teach people what they should
think of God and how they should treat each other.
But there was much more he wanted to say. He needed
more time to help people see the truth about God and
one another, as he saw it. And now perhaps he was
to have no time. Then the question was, would these
young men who had known him best carry on his
work? Would they be brave enough to face opposition as he had done and as they must do? It would
be a terrible thing if all that he had tried to do should
come to nothing.

Such thoughts came to Jesus. But with them came
the confidence that the young men would not fail.
His work would not fail. Only they must feel how
much might depend on them. And so Jesus spoke to
them suggesting that they might not meet together
in this way again. Finally he took some of the bread
from the table and keeping a piece himself he passed
the rest of it to the young men, saying to them: " Eat
this bread tonight with me now. Then when you meet
with one another again, think of how we have eaten
here."

After that he took a cup of the wine which they
drank instead of water at this feast, and he asked them
to drink with him so that in later days in their meals
together they would recall him and what he had done
for them.

They did not understand all that Jesus was thinking about. Only after many days did they understand. But they felt it was a most solemn time as they joined with Jesus in eating the bread and drinking the wine. Nor did they ever forget what he told them. Even to this day the Christian churches from time to time hold a service called "The Communion," in which they repeat the action of that long-ago night. And when people thus recall Jesus and his teaching and his brave, great life, they are helped, let us hope, to believe and to do the things he taught.

QUESTIONS AND TOPICS FOR STUDY

What was to take place on Thursday evening of that same week? What plans had Jesus made for keeping the feast with his friends? Why did he wish to keep this a secret? How did the two sent on ahead find the place?

Where did Jesus plan to spend the night? What did he wish to accomplish with his young men before danger should overtake him? What did he want to make them feel? How did he go about this?

Why would his friends remember him when they met together thereafter? Do you think they understood all Jesus said and did at that last feast? Did they ever come to understand his meaning? When?

What service like this last Passover do Christian churches still hold? Why do they hold such a service? How does it help Christians today?

Further Discoveries

Read how Jesus taught his disciples a lesson in service. (John 13: 1-17; Luke 22: 24-27.) What commandment did Jesus leave his disciples? (John 13: 34, 35; 14: 15, 21, 23, 24; 15: 9, 10, 12-17.) What promise did Jesus give his friends? (John 14: 16-19, 25-27.)

Something to Do

Record in your diary what took place on Thursday evening of the Passover week, and what impression it left on all the disciples of Jesus.

CHAPTER XVIII
Judas the Traitor

MEANWHILE one of the young men had left the room. Judas had heard what he had waited to hear, just where Jesus was to spend the night. This was the thing the enemies of Jesus wanted to know, and they were ready to pay anyone who would tell them. Through the dark streets of the city hurried this man whose name was so soon to be known for one of the worst deeds in history. It was very quiet. The busy crowds were all indoors in attendance upon the feasts. Here and there lights gleamed through the windows of rooms where the tables were set for the Passover. No one noticed him. He reached quickly the house he sought. It was that of one of the chief Jewish citizens, a priest in the temple.

A servant at the door took his name, went away, and returning a moment later led him to where the master of the house was seated.

"Well," said the man to Judas, "have you found out what we want to know? We are ready to pay you."

What a poor sad business it was! But Judas had gone too far to turn back. He must go on now to complete the evil task. He did not care much for the money. He told himself again that no great harm would come to Jesus, but he would be stopped from his teaching. In his disappointment Judas wanted to bring this about.

"Yes," he said, "in an hour the Teacher and his young men will be in the Garden of Gethsemane on the side of the mountain."

The thing was done. Nothing could save Jesus now unless Judas should return and warn him. But Judas had no idea of doing this. In fact, the great officer of the temple, with whom he was speaking, intended that Judas should do something more to earn the money to be paid him.

"You will receive what I promised," he said to Judas, "but I wish you to be with the police I am sending to arrest Jesus. They may not know him, especially in the dark. Go to him and kiss him on the cheek when you see him. This will point him out. Do not fail. Now you can go."

Then he called one of his servants and told him to see to it that the men who kept order about the temple, and others who might be collected quickly, were sent at once to the Garden of Gethsemane. There they were to find and make Jesus a prisoner and bring him to the house. It took some little time to make up this company, but finally it was done and they marched out through one of the east gates of the city, down the steep hill into the ravine where the little stream called the Brook Kedron flowed, and then a short distance up the other hillslope to where the dark mass of the olive orchard could be made out in the night.

———————

Meanwhile the Passover celebration in the room

where we left Jesus and his young men had come to
its ending. They sang together a hymn as its closing
act. Then silently they went out into the dark streets,
through the city gate, down to the ravine, and climbing the hill they passed in among the trees. It was
very late. Jesus knew that his young men were tired
and sleepy, and so he told all but three of them to
take what rest they could under the stars. These three,
Peter, James, John, he asked to go a little apart from
the others.

"It is well," he said to them, "to keep watch. Be
on your guard for a little while."

Then he himself went still farther away. He was
not afraid but he felt certain that danger was close at
hand. He had noted when Judas left the room. In
an instant he suspected why he left. But there was
nothing further he could do. He had no other friends
near-by. There was no safe place anywhere in the
city bounds. He was ready to meet the worst, feeling,
as we have seen, that even if he were killed the work
he had tried to do would not fail.

And yet, all alone in the darkness, how natural to
feel the weight of the coming danger, pain, loss and
sorrow. The power of the great city over the ravine
on its hilltop was to be used against him. And he had
only tried to do for the people fine and beautiful
things. Do you wonder if he longed, oh, so earnestly!
that he might escape, go back to the pleasant hills of
Galilee, and find there safety and quiet? Yet he knew

it could not be. He was determined not to retreat. And in his great need he turned to God the Father, about whom he had taught and in whose help he trusted. There was no one to listen and hear his words, but from all we know of him we may be sure that he prayed thus:

"O God, if in any way I can be saved from the great danger that threatens, I pray that I may be. But if there is no way but for me to suffer, help me with thy strength."

And as we shall now see, God did give him help and strength.

QUESTIONS AND TOPICS FOR STUDY

Who left the room during the Passover supper? Why did he leave? Where did he go? What was he to receive for his information? Did he think any real harm would come to Jesus because of his deed? Did he know he was doing wrong? How wrong do you suppose he felt it was?

Did you ever do something that you felt was only slightly wrong? Perhaps nothing much ever came of it; perhaps it turned out far worse than you thought it would. For how much of the trouble were you responsible—for the little you knew you were doing, or for everything that happened as a result of your deed? How can we keep the very bad results from happening? (If you have never had any such experience of your own, make up a story of a boy or a girl who did have. Perhaps the person told what he thought was a little falsehood, and somebody came to great harm because of it; perhaps he disobeyed in something he felt unimportant and brought great trouble to himself and others because of it.)

It may have been that way with Judas. What may have been his reason for wishing to have Jesus arrested? What was to be the sign whereby he would show the officers which was Jesus? Who were sent to arrest Jesus?

What did Jesus and his friends do after the Passover supper? (Mark 14:26.) Who went apart with Jesus? Of what might Jesus have been thinking when alone in the garden? (Luke 22: 39-42.) Why did he think his work would not fail if danger came to him? Where did he perhaps long to go? Why didn't he?

Further Discoveries

Read in your Bible about Judas. (Matthew 26: 14-25; Mark 14: 10, 11; Luke 22: 1-6; John 13: 21-30.)

Something to Do

Write in your diary your impression of what took place on this night, up to the time Jesus went into the garden with his friends.

CHAPTER XIX

THE GREAT HOUR IN THE GARDEN

ANXIOUS and wakeful with the sense of the great danger that surrounded them, he walked back the few steps to where he had left the three young men keeping watch, to see if they had heard or seen anything. He found them *fast asleep*. The peril which Jesus knew was so near, they did not realize at all. Weary with the long day their eyelids had closed almost as soon as they found comfortable places to rest under the olive trees. As Jesus softly awakened them, they looked up at him with surprise and shame at having fallen asleep. "Be on your guard," he said quietly. "I know you want to help me, but your strength fails you."

Then he left them and again he went away a little distance by himself. Once more the thought of the terrible danger which threatened his life came over him. Should he run from it? The darkness would aid him. Beneath its protection he could escape over the mountain. Before morning he would be safe at Bethany. Thence he could go back to Nazareth. No one would follow him. But if he did, if he left Jerusalem, breaking the custom of spending the Passover night in the city, if he deserted his work of teaching, men would forget not only him but what he had told them. They would say he was afraid of the priests and politicians in Jerusalem. His influence and the influence of his words would be gone forever.

All this Jesus considered and with another prayer to God for help, he made the decision to stay, no matter what happened to him, no matter what it cost him. When we think of the great moments in the history of our world, we must think of that midnight beneath the olive trees in Gethsemane. And when we think of the results that have followed these heroic decisions, we place that of Jesus first and most important of all.

With no thought of sleep for himself, Jesus returned to his three young men. Do you suppose you would have been more faithful than they? It is easy to resolve to do something. Quite often it is exceedingly hard to carry out the resolve. Peter and James and John loved Jesus, they were anxious about him; but they did not understand how bitter were his enemies, and they were very tired. So it was that Jesus found them again sleeping. He did not waken them this time, but once more walked away by himself under the dark branches. Then once again he returned to them, this time to waken not only the three but the other eight who were asleep not far away.

In the quiet night air Jesus had caught the sound of metal striking against stone. Listening he had heard the movement of many feet. The light of a torch, guarded but not altogether concealed, gleamed on the road up from the ravine. And then, just as he wakened his young men and they sought to collect their thoughts after their heavy sleep, the company of temple police and men picked up in the streets of Jerusalem cast all attempt at secrecy aside and noisily crowded in among the olive trees.

Foremost with the officer in charge walked Judas. And now he was to do the last terrible thing. It was necessary that Jesus should be pointed out, for there was no plan to arrest anyone else. Straight up to Jesus Judas walked. It was a common custom of that day and that land for one man when meeting another to kiss him on the cheek, just as two men who meet in our country today shake hands and say "How do you do?" In this way Judas greeted Jesus.

"Teacher, teacher," he called out and kissed him.

At once the crowd pushed forward. The officer took hold of Jesus and directed two members of the temple police to guard him carefully. For just a few moments Jesus' young men offered resistance. But they were a few against many. They were caught by surprise and unprepared. Jesus knew it would be hopeless to fight. Moreover, he did not intend to fight. He was going to try a harder way that called for more courage but would be better for his cause at last. He spoke to his young men, therefore, and told them not to offer resistance. Then he spoke to the officer of the temple police:

"Did you need to come after me with this big force

of armed men? I have been in the city every day. Why
did you not arrest me there?"

They had no answer. But they were strong enough
to do as they intended. The officer in command gave
his orders and the march back to the city began.

QUESTIONS AND TOPICS FOR STUDY

What had happened in the meantime to the three friends with
Jesus? What did Jesus say to them? Do you think they knew the
danger? (Matthew 26:31-35.)

What might people say if Jesus ran away? How long would
they probably remember his teachings? Could he keep on with his
work? What success might he have later if he ran away now?
Why was this one of the greatest moments in history?

Did the three friends stay awake the second time? Why not?
What happened as Jesus awakened all those with him? Who was
in this crowd? What did Judas do? (Luke 22:47, 48.)

What happened to Jesus? Did Jesus' friends try to protect him?
Why was Jesus unwilling to have them fight for him? What did
Jesus say to the officer who arrested him? Why had they not taken
him when he was at Jerusalem in the daytime?

Further Discoveries

Read about this night in your Bible. (Matthew 26:45-56;
Mark 14:41-50; Luke 22:47-53; John 18:1-11.)

Something to Do

What are you going to add to your diary about what took place
in the garden of Gethsemane? How can you describe the temptation
Jesus may have had to go away? How will you say he overcame it?
How can you compare it with an earlier temptation to be untrue
to his work? How did his victory then help him now?

CHAPTER XX

JESUS A PRISONER

THE place to which Jesus was taken was the house of one of the chief men connected with the temple, who was called the high priest. There is nobody in our life today who has a place just like that which he filled in Jerusalem. He had great power but it was limited by one thing which we must remember. The Romans had conquered Palestine with their armies and ruled the land. They left many rights to the people of Jerusalem and the officials whom they chose, but in the most important matters the governor appointed by the emperor of Rome settled what was to be done. Only he could order anyone to be put to death. The governor at this time was a man by the name of Pontius Pilate.

If we remember these things we can better understand why matters happened as they did. First of all Jesus' enemies must find Jesus to be guilty of something for which he could be put to death. Then they must go to the governor, show him what they had discovered and persuade him to give orders condemning Jesus to death. There are thus what we might call three chapters in this closing part of Jesus' life story. There is the trial before the high priest and his associates. Then there is the trial before Pontius Pilate, the governor, where the high priest presents his charge.

And lastly comes the terrible carrying out of this sentence of death.

Jesus was led by his captors into a room where the high priest was seated with other important men of the city. They were all members of the group called Sadducees.

In a trial, as you may know, there must be besides the judge and the prisoner, the witnesses who tell what they know about the prisoner. In this trial of Jesus certain men had been found whose words might be used against him. But the difficulty that his enemies found was that what one witness said did not agree with what another said. Moreover, the thing that they declared Jesus said was not anything for which he could be put to death. So they had to see if they could not get him to say something then and there which would condemn him.

At first Jesus made no answer to their questions. He knew that these men before whom he had been brought were bent on killing him. He did not know of a friend who could help him as he stood there all alone. But his courage never failed and he would not let his cruel enemies trick him. So for a while he kept a steady silence. At last, however, the high priest asked him a question which he felt he must answer.

"Are you the anointed one sent from God?"

Jesus felt that God had sent him to speak His truth. And he felt also that he was really the great leader whom his people had long looked for and had ex-

pected God to send them. He had not come just as
they expected. But he had come to do even greater
things than they had dreamed would happen. And
so it was that to this question he made reply, saying,
"I am the leader appointed by God."

The minute he said this the high priest sprang out
of his seat. He pretended to be surprised and shocked
beyond all words at first. Then he cried out,

"We do not need any further word. He has condemned himself."

Then with great excitement they all voted that
Jesus had said something for which he ought to die.
Probably you are surprised that this answer of Jesus
could seem to anyone a bad thing to say. At least,
how could anyone be put to death for saying it? The
fact is, we must say again, these men had made up
their minds to kill Jesus. They were so afraid that he
would stir up some trouble which would end in hurt-
ing them that they were bent on finding any sort of
excuse for carrying out their purpose. It is also true
that what Jesus had said might be called by those who
did not believe him as something said against their
religion. According to their Jewish law anyone who
did this could be punished with death. Probably they
knew Jesus intended to help and not to harm their
religion. They knew he had done nothing to deserve
death, but to kill him was the surest way to end all
trouble, they thought. It was the safest way for them,
and so they all cried out that he should be put to death.

QUESTIONS AND TOPICS FOR STUDY

Where was Jesus taken? How much power did the high priest have? What kind of power was it? (Read in Leviticus 10: 8-11, about some of the duties of priests.) Who alone could order prisoners to be put to death? What was the name of the Roman governor at this time? What would Jesus' enemies have to do before he could be condemned?

Where was Jesus first led? Who was there? (Matthew 26: 57.) What was the matter with what the witnesses said? (Mark 14: 55-59.) What ancient law was broken in this trial? (Exodus 20: 16.) What did his enemies try to get Jesus to do? What question did they finally ask Jesus? (Mark 14: 60, 61.) What was his reply? (Mark 14: 62.) What did he mean when he said he was a leader appointed by God? What did the high priest do when he heard Jesus say this? (Mark 14: 63.) Why could Jesus be put to death for what he had said? Did his enemies really think he was a bad man? What were they afraid of?

What do you think of this kind of trial? Can you think of any ways whereby one may be sure of justice during a trial? What kind of laws are needed for justice? What kind of judges are needed?

Something to Do

Record the trial of Jesus, making comments on the justice of it, and how it might have been conducted fairly.

CHAPTER XXI

Two Young Men Who Failed

THE group with the high priest could condemn Jesus but they did not have the power to give any orders for his death. They must now take Jesus to the Roman governor. But before we follow them thither let us stop to recall two of Jesus' young men, one of whom already had been false to him, the other of whom was about to be. We will think of the latter first.

Jesus' enemies could not go to Pilate until morning. So in those hours when the night was passing but the dawn had not yet quite come, Jesus remained a prisoner in the house of the high priest. It was during this time that something happened which shows how easy it is for the bravest purpose to fail.

Some time during the early evening, when Jesus had been talking with his disciples, he had told them something of the danger he believed to be near. Peter, always quick to speak and act, said boldly that although everyone else should leave Jesus, he would never do so. And then Jesus, knowing how much harder was to be the experience before them than any of them knew, said to Peter,

" Before the cock crow " (that is, before the morning comes) " you will fail me."

When Jesus had been taken to the house of the high priest most of his young men had gone off in the darkness. Peter and John had followed at a distance. The house was built on the slope of the hill at the top of which was the temple. There was an outer courtyard, then an inner courtyard. Around this the main part of the house was built, the rooms leading off a gallery. In the center of the court a fire of charcoal had been lighted, for the spring night was cool.

Ordinarily Peter and John would not have been permitted to enter the house. But it so happened that John knew one of the maids who admitted visitors, and with her help they gained their entrance. As they were passing in she thought she recognized Peter and said to him, "Are you also one of his young men?" Peter usually so bold, but troubled and fearful about Jesus, was caught by surprise. Almost before he knew what he was saying he had cried out, "No, no."

The two men now came into the courtyard where the fire was burning. They drew closer to it, for they were chilled and weary. The dancing flames lighted up their faces as they stood there. One of the servants of the high priest looked up and, having seen Peter somewhere with Jesus, thought he recognized him.

"Are you not one of Jesus' young men?" he said. And poor Peter, held by his former lie, was guilty of another: "No," he declared.

Once more, shortly afterwards as he moved restlessly about the courtyard, yet another servant saw him and asked the question. And once more Peter denied knowing Jesus.

It was nearly dawn by this time and somewhere

near-by a rooster crowed loudly. Peter heard it. At
the same time looking up at the gallery around the
courtyard he caught sight of Jesus as he was led along
from one room to another. His proud promise and
Jesus' warning came back to his mind. When he
thought of it and saw Jesus alone and friendless and
felt how he had been false and cowardly, he covered
his head with his cloak and cried like a little child.

Was that the end for Peter? Oh, no. Peter was not
false or cowardly at heart. He was only so because
he had not been on his guard. Like all of us at times
he thought he was braver and stronger than he really
was. And he needed this terrible lesson. He learned
it well. Not long afterward, as we shall see before we
reach the end of the story, he showed himself the
bravest of the brave.

And what about Judas, that other young man who
was false to Jesus? He had done his evil deed after
thinking about it and planning for it. He could not
give the excuse that he had not meant to harm Jesus;
for he knew that that was just what he had planned,
even although he had not meant to cause Jesus' death.
When he found out what was going to happen through
his action, he would have given anything in the world
to undo what he had done. But it was too late. He
even tried to get the high priest to take back the money
given him. The sight of it was hateful to him. But
the high priest would not do this. He did not care
how Judas felt. We have one last sad picture of this

young man as, standing in the high priest's house before this official and some of his associates, Judas
throws down the coins he cannot keep and goes out
into the night. It was thought that he killed himself.
Some said he did it in one way, others thought it was
in a different way. We never can know what really
happened. Alas for him! We can never forget what
he did.

QUESTIONS AND TOPICS FOR STUDY

What had Peter promised Jesus earlier in the evening? What
was Jesus' reply? (Matthew 26: 31-35.) What happened to the
young men with Jesus when he was arrested? (Matthew 26: 56.)
Where did Peter and John go? (John 18: 15.) What did one of
the maids say to Peter? (John 18: 16, 17.) What was his answer?
Where did he go next? (John 18: 18.) What did one of the other
servants ask him? What was his reply this time? (John 18: 25.)
Why? Do you think he was afraid to say he was with Jesus? Do
you think he thought he had to stick to his first lie? (Have you
ever heard it said that one lie leads to another? Why is this so?
Give an example.) Was Peter questioned again about knowing
Jesus? (John 18: 26.) What happened then? (John 18: 27.)
How did Peter happen to see Jesus soon afterward? What did
Jesus do? What did Peter do? (Luke 22: 61, 62.)

Why did Peter need to discover his weakness? Why was Judas
worse than Peter? What did Judas do with the money the priest
had given him for betraying Jesus? What happened to Judas in
the end? For what is he remembered? (Read about the remorse
and death of Judas, in Matthew 27: 1-10.)

Something to Do

Continue your diary by recording what happened to Peter and
Judas, giving a character sketch of each.

CHAPTER XXII

JESUS AND A ROMAN GOVERNOR

AS soon as it was late enough in the morning for the Roman governor to be ready to hold his court, the enemies of Jesus gave orders that their men who were guarding Jesus should lead him to the house of Pilate. The governor had never heard of Jesus and knew nothing about what had happened. When he looked at Jesus standing before him, so quiet, so unlike any criminal he had ever judged, he was greatly surprised. And he asked at once, "Of what do you accuse this man?"

They began to tell him of what Jesus had said. But Pilate was only inclined the more to favor Jesus. He did not like the Jewish people over whom he was set to keep order. He thought them a very troublesome lot, constantly quarreling over small things and objecting to what seemed to him of no account at all. He had no respect for their religion. So when they told him that Jesus claimed to be sent from God, he was on the point of sending them away to settle their dispute by themselves and not bother him with it.

This, however, was just what the high priest and his friends did not wish to have happen, because only Pilate could order Jesus' death. And so they changed their accusation against Jesus. "He claims," they said to Pilate, "to be King of the Jews."

This was a different matter. If Jesus was trying to become king, he must have been plotting against Rome. It was Pilate's first business to check such attempts and to punish mercilessly those who took any part in them. He was obliged to consider this charge, however much he disliked the high priest and all his group, and however much he was inclined to respect and, in a careless way, to admire Jesus. And so he had to listen while they told him whatever they could think of saying to prove what a dangerous man Jesus was.

Jesus himself said nothing. He knew how useless it was to contradict their false statements, for they would declare he did not tell the truth. Pilate was surprised that he kept silence and asked him several times if he had nothing to say. But he only shook his head and made no reply. And yet Pilate felt sure that he was not the bad, dangerous man he was said to be. Pilate knew enough of men to judge about Jesus correctly. Why then, you say, did he not set Jesus free at once? Because he was afraid to do right. He wanted to remain governor, and he feared lest word might be sent to Rome that when a rebel leader had been delivered to him as a prisoner he had not punished him. This would be regarded as a fault so great that the emperor would make another man governor in his place. Even if this did not happen there was the chance that the high priest's party could stir up much trouble in Jerusalem which he would have to stop.

Perhaps many would be killed. It would seem as though he were not able to keep order in Palestine. For this he would be put out of office.

Now it so happened that just at this time the man who governed Jesus' home province of Galilee was in Jerusalem on a visit. As the priests were telling what Jesus had done they spoke of his coming from Galilee. The moment Pilate heard that, he saw a chance to get out of the unpleasant task set for him. Jesus ought to be judged by this other ruler. It was somewhat as though a man charged with doing wrong in Massachusetts were found to be a citizen of Ohio, and as though the governor of Ohio, happening to be on a visit to Boston, were asked by the governor of Massachusetts to take charge of the prisoner. Pilate at once ordered soldiers to march Jesus over to the house where the other ruler was staying.

This man, also, whose name was Herod, had never seen Jesus but he had heard of him and was curious to see him. He hoped that perhaps Jesus would do for him one of the wonderful things rumor had brought to his ears. But he was disappointed. Jesus would not try to be free by doing what was like buying Herod's favor. The priests had come along to accuse him in this new court. After a while, angry at Jesus' refusal to speak, Herod's followers put on him a cloak of the colors kings wore. Then they made fun of him. Finally, not wanting the trouble of settling the matter, Herod sent him back to the Roman governor.

There was just one other thing Pilate could do. He had remembered that every Passover time it was a custom for the governor to set free some prisoner. It so happened that there was in the prison just then a man who had been a highway robber and who had also tried to stir up a revolution. He had been caught and sentenced to die. Between this man, whose name was Barabbas, and Jesus, Pilate thought there would be no question if he were to offer to set one or the other free.

QUESTIONS AND TOPICS FOR STUDY

Where was Jesus taken the next morning? How did Pilate feel toward the Jews whom he ruled? What did he think of their religion? Had Pilate ever seen or heard of Jesus? What did he probably think as he looked at Jesus standing there?

Of what did the Jewish rulers accuse the prisoner? (Luke 23: 1, 2.) Compare this with what they had accused him of before. Why did they have to change their accusation to make Jesus a criminal in the sight of the Roman governor? What did Pilate think after hearing the accusation? (Luke 23: 3, 4.) Why was he obliged to hear the case? (Luke 23: 5.)

What would happen to Jesus if his enemies could prove their accusation? What did Jesus say to it? (Mark 15: 3-5.) Why did not Pilate set him free? What might happen if word reached Rome that the governor had not punished a rebel? What else might happen to cause trouble if Jesus were set free?

What did Pilate hear about at this time? Where did he send Jesus? (Luke 23: 6, 7.) Why did not Herod settle the case? What had he expected to see Jesus do? (Luke 23: 8-10.) Why did Jesus do nothing? What did the followers of the king do to Jesus? (Luke 23: 11.) What result came of Pilate's sending Jesus to Herod? (Luke 23: 12.)

What did Pilate remember to offer the people at the Passover time? (Matthew 27: 15.) Who was Barabbas? (Mark 15: 7.) Whom did Pilate think the people would choose to set free? What message did Pilate's wife send to him? (Matthew 27: 19.)

What would you have done, if you had been Pilate?

Something to Do

Record in your diary what happened when Jesus was sent to Pilate and Herod.

CHAPTER XXIII

Jesus or Barabbas?

YOU must understand that what had so far occurred had taken place within Pilate's house.
But while the time was passing a large crowd had
gathered together outside. Jesus had attracted enough
attention by what he had been saying in the temple
courts during the week to make the news of his arrest
an interesting story. One by one or by small groups
many people had been drawn together. There were
great numbers of pilgrims who had little to do and
were ready for any excitement. There was also the
usual number of idle people in Jerusalem who, having no regular business, welcomed anything that
promised to amuse them. With these there were
doubtless a few who were Jesus' real friends and were
greatly troubled at the danger threatening him. But
to far the larger number Jesus seemed just a man from
up in the north country, who had come down to Jerusalem to the Passover feast, had talked and acted
foolishly, and had thereby gotten into trouble. If in a
crowd of such people, who know little about what is
going on, there are a few shrewd men who act as
leaders, these few can stir up much excitement; and
the crowd can be led to do what no member of it would
do by himself.

As soon as they saw the people collecting that morning, the enemies of Jesus had made it a point to start

stories about him and to give out the impression that
a very dangerous man was on trial before Pilate. As
time went by the people got more and more impatient,
and it was increasingly easy to get them to do what
their leaders wanted them to do. As soon as the priests
heard Pilate's offer, they at once sent out the word
through the crowd that they should shout for Barabbas. It is possible that some number of them may have
known Barabbas, and were all ready to hurrah for him
as a man that had tried to start trouble for the hated
Romans.

The choice between Jesus and Barabbas was to be
made by the people. Such was the custom. In order,
therefore, to carry out the plan he had in mind, Pilate
brought Jesus out upon a little balcony overlooking
the street. Then speaking in a loud voice he said:

"You have a custom at this feast that I shall grant
a pardon to some one man, charged with wrongdoing
against the government. You have brought here this
man Jesus. Sometime ago Barabbas was arrested and
condemned as a rebel. Today I will free one of these
men. Which shall it be?"

And then it was that the crowd, led by the
agents of the priests, shouted out loudly, "Barabbas!
Barabbas!"

Pilate was silent for a moment. He had counted on
settling this disagreeable business by his clever plan.
He was so sure that Jesus was innocent of any serious
wrongdoing that he simply did not even then realize

how vindictive was the spirit of the priests. We can catch his astonishment in the question that broke from him,

"What then do you wish to do with this man who, you say, claims to be your king?"

The priests had made the crowd ready for just such a chance as this. Their shout went up, "Crucify him, crucify him!"

Thus was the question forced on Pilate. Now was the time for him to show courage as Jesus had done. How different would have been his story if he had only stood by what he knew to be right! But he miserably failed. He gave in to the priests. Although he despised them he would not oppose them. He gave the order that Jesus should first be scourged and then be crucified.

QUESTIONS AND TOPICS FOR STUDY

Why had a large crowd been gathering outside of Pilate's house? (Mark 15:6-8.) What did they know of Jesus? Were any of Jesus' friends there? How might the enemies of Jesus be able to stir up such a crowd against Jesus? What did the priests do as soon as they heard about Pilate's decision to let the people choose their prisoner? (Matthew 27:20, and Mark 15:11.)

Where did Pilate take Jesus? What did he say to the people? What was the result? Why was Pilate surprised? What did he ask of the crowd? What was their reply? How might Pilate have showed his courage then? What did he do? Why do you think he failed to stand for what he knew was right? Of what was he afraid? (John 19:12.) How did he try to ease his conscience? (Matthew 27:22-25.)

For You to Think About

Why do people often put their own interests before justice? Why do they often think of themselves before others? How much courage does it take to stand up for the right regardless of consequences to oneself? Do you know of anyone who dared do this?

For You to Decide

How can we have courage such as Jesus had? When must we begin to practice it? Can we act in a selfish and cowardly way part of the time and then be brave when a real test of our courage comes? Why not? How can we be ready for heroism? Why was Peter caught unprepared? How can we be practicing each day?

CHAPTER XXIV

JESUS AND THE CROSS

SCOURGING meant being beaten on the back with a terrible sort of whip, to the cords of which were fastened pieces of metal that tore the flesh. Soldiers took Jesus to their guardhouse, stripped off his upper garments, tied him to a pillar in the court-yard, and one of their number struck him again and again. Then over his bleeding back they threw once more the robe which Herod had caused him to wear to make fun of him. These rough men did not hate Jesus. He was just a prisoner they could treat any way they wished. Because they had become naturally cruel through their life as soldiers, it was good sport for them to cause Jesus all the pain they could. They had heard that he was going to be put to death because he had claimed to be a king. Some one of them had a small branch of a tree with long, sharp thorns grow-ing from it. They took this, brought the ends together, and pressed it down on Jesus' head to look like a crown. Another one of them took a branch of a palm tree and thrust it into Jesus' hand as if it were a scepter. Then they crowded about him, striking him roughly and shouting to him to name the one who had given the blow.

Deserted by all his friends, alone in the hands of these brutal soldiers, Jesus suffered the pain of the scourging and the mockery that followed with the

steadiest bravery. He had had only the desire to help
people live better and happier lives. For doing this it
now seemed that all the world was turned against him.
His heart might well have been broken by what had
happened. You could not blame him if he had lost
courage in the face of his all-powerful enemies. He
had had no sleep or rest since Wednesday night. It
was now nearly noon of Friday. Yet almost overcome
by the pain of the scourging, weary, despairing of any
help from his friends, he faced his enemies with
dauntless spirit.

And now tiring of the savage play they had been
carrying on, the Roman soldiers made ready to carry
out the governor's orders to put Jesus to death by cru-
cifying him. This was a form of death long since given
up as too cruel. A heavy piece of timber was nailed
crosswise to another yet heavier and longer piece.
Then the condemned man was held down, his arms
were stretched out along the crosspiece, through his
hands were driven great spikes, and his feet were
nailed to the upright beam in the same fearful fashion.
The cross was then set down into a hole prepared for
it. There it stood with its victim until he died.

The cross on which Jesus was to die had been made
ready. It was part of the custom in putting a man to
death to compel him to carry to the place of execution
the cross on which he was to die. This was a low hill
just outside the walls. A guard of soldiers was formed.
Jesus was ordered to lift the cross upon his shoulders

and the procession started towards the gate of the city. Such of the crowd as had lingered around the guard-house where the scourging took place followed after them. So weak had Jesus become as a result of the way he had been treated that he fell beneath the weight of the cross, and it was impossible for him to go on. Seeing this the officer in charge of the soldiers ordered one of them to seize some man in the crowd and make him bear the cross. The order was carried out. A man by the name of Simon, who had come in from a near-by village to spend the day in Jerusalem, was dragged up to where Jesus had fallen and made to lift up the cross. Then once again they moved on, through the Damascus Gate of the city to the hill.

Two other men who had been condemned to death were to be crucified with Jesus. One after the other each was nailed to his cross, which with its load of suffering was then set into the ground. That of Jesus was the middle one of the three. His clothes, which had been stripped from him, were divided among the soldiers. Far on the outskirts of the crowd were certain women who had believed in him. His mother also had followed to the place. His young men, horrified, frightened and in despair, had gone out of the city or were in hiding there. The sun beat down on Jesus and his two companions on the cross. Thirst and heat increased the agony in their pain-racked bodies.

QUESTIONS AND TOPICS FOR STUDY

Why do you think it was the custom to scourge a prisoner before putting him to death? Who was it that beat Jesus? Why did they think this was sport? What kind of men were the Roman soldiers? What made them hard and cruel? What did they put on Jesus after beating him? How did Jesus stand all this pain and disappointment? Why do you think he was able to be so brave?

Where was Jesus finally put to death? Who carried the cross for him? Why? Through which gate of the city did they pass?

Who else was crucified at the same time? What was done with Jesus' clothes? Were any of Jesus' friends near?

Further Discoveries

Read about these events in your Bible, comparing the different accounts. (Matthew 27: 26-44; Mark 15: 16-32; Luke 23: 25-43; John 19: 1-27.)

Something to Do

Tell something of the mob which gathered about after Jesus had been tried, then of the procession outside the city and what took place there.

CHAPTER XXV

THE DEATH OF JESUS

ALTHOUGH the pain from the crucifixion was fearful, it usually happened that the poor victim of it lived some time, dying at last from exhaustion. But Jesus lived only a few hours after being nailed to the cross. He had suffered much from the cruelty of the soldiers. This, however, does not altogether explain his early release from the pain. He had been spending his whole strength so tirelessly in the work he had sought to do that when it all seemed to end in the triumph of his enemies, the thought broke down his will to live and after three hours he was dead.

But in those three hours some things happened which were never to be forgotten. The two robbers crucified with Jesus were rough men who had lived hard lives. One of them died as he had lived, railing at those who punished him and at Jesus.

"If you are God's appointed one," he cried, "why don't you save yourself and us?"

And when Jesus made no reply he broke out against him with oaths.

But the other robber was deeply moved by Jesus' calm quiet courage. He felt that Jesus was indeed a great and good man.

"Be quiet!" he cried out. "Will you not be decent before you die? Can't you tell that this man is not like us? We get what we deserve, but he has done nothing wrong."

And then turning to Jesus he spoke to him with respect and great longing: "Master, do not forget me when you are happy in the other world."

Jesus had been silent when men had been cruel, harsh and false to him. But now when a man cried out to him for help, he did not think of his own suffering.

"Today," he said, "whatever good comes to me I will share with you."

A few soldiers lingered near to see that no one came to rescue the dying men. Curiosity-seekers from the city walked out to the hill and looked at the crosses and especially at that where Jesus hung. Most of these people were careless and indifferent. Some of the priests were there, gloating over the fact that they had gotten out of the way the young man who would have turned people against them and lessened their power.

"He claimed to help people," they said with a sneer, "let him get out of his own trouble now."

As the weary minutes passed, Jesus' spirits sank beneath the awful burden of his pain.

"Oh God," he murmured once, "why have you left me?"

But then, even as he grew weaker and weaker, he felt sure God had not forgotten him, and at last just before he died he spoke again:

"Father, into thy hands I give myself."

There was a Roman officer who had been left in

charge of the soldiers and who had seen how patiently Jesus had borne the pain, how steadily he had faced death, how heroically he had died. Now that he saw Jesus was dead, he could not keep back an expression of perfect respect, and he said to those standing near by, " He was certainly a good man."

The next day was the rest day, the Sabbath, as it was called. No work of any sort could be done. The whole business of the crucifixion must be finished before dark.

The Roman soldiers would be glad enough to hurry matters for their own sake if not to please the Jews. Jesus having died, the death of the two robbers was hastened. Then came the question of what to do with the bodies. What happened to those of the robbers we do not know, but for that of Jesus an unexpected friend came forward. This new friend was a member of one of the wealthy families of Jerusalem. He was connected in an official way with the very group of priests who had brought about Jesus' death. But he had for a long time admired Jesus and felt he was teaching what was true. Before this, he had not come out openly as his friend. Now, however, he came to the help of Jesus' friends, the good women who had followed even to the hill of crucifixion. But for him they would have been powerless to have cared for the poor broken body of Jesus.

Just at the very foot of the hill was a little garden.

The hill was bare, bleak, forbidding, but the garden was green and restful, a little place of peace so near to one of brutal death. It belonged to this man whose name was Joseph. Out of a ledge of rock which bounded the garden on one side had been cut a tomb. It had never been used but was all ready for a body to be placed within it. To save all trouble, Joseph went to the governor to ask if he might bury the body of Jesus, and Pilate said that he might. Then Joseph and the good women had Jesus' body carried down into the garden. They washed away the blood of the wounds, cared for the body as they knew how to do, and then as the evening shadows were falling over the little garden they laid it tenderly within the tomb. Across the entrance was set a heavy piece of stone, and as night came over the city they went to their homes.

QUESTIONS AND TOPICS FOR STUDY

Why did Jesus not live as long as the thieves? What did one of them say to him? Why did Jesus not answer? Why did he summon strength to answer the other thief? How did the priests feel when they saw Jesus was out of their way?

If you were called upon to suffer in some terrible way, would you feel that God was near you? Why do people sometimes lose faith in God when trouble comes? Why did Jesus feel at the end that God was near? What did one of the soldiers say when Jesus died?

Why was it the Jewish custom to complete the execution of criminals before the Sabbath? Who asked Pilate for the privilege of caring for the body of Jesus? Who helped Joseph bury Jesus according to the Jewish customs? Where was he laid to rest? What was set across the entrance of the tomb?

Further Discoveries

What happened the day Jesus was crucified? (Matthew 27: 45, 51.) Can you imagine the effect this had upon the people? What may they have thought about the earthquake? What do you suppose Pilate was thinking? (John 19: 7, 8.) What did some of the soldiers think? (Matthew 27: 54.) What did Jesus cry out? (Matthew 27: 46.) Did Jesus really feel forsaken by God at the last? (Luke 23: 46.) What was Jesus' attitude toward those who killed him? (Luke 23: 33, 34.)

Something to Do

Complete your diary up to this point. What will you have to say of the courage of Jesus compared with that of Peter and of Pilate? What will you decide gave Jesus strength to bear his pain and sorrow? How will you describe the feelings of different groups of people at the death of Jesus—of the priests, of the Romans, of the friends of Jesus?

CHAPTER XXVI

AFTERWARDS

YOU would naturally think that we had now reached the end of the story. The brave young man with his wonderful teaching about God and the way we should act towards one another has been put to death. Enemies who hated him for the very good he did have defeated his plans. Surely his memory will be tenderly kept by those who loved him. The words he spoke will not be forgotten, nor the deeds he did. But his followers are few. They have no power. They are much discouraged and they are broken-hearted. It cannot be that they will gather together soon or that they will have much influence when they do.

This is what you would expect to be true. But this is not what happened. Something occurred that changed all this. Within a not very long time these young men who had followed Jesus are talking about him in the temple and on the streets of Jerusalem. They are calling people to become his followers. They are going out through Palestine with his story. And hundreds of people are listening and saying, "We should like to be his followers."

Then the same group that caused Jesus' death begins to arrest and punish those who become known as believers in him. Some are put in prison; others are put to death. But all this only sends the story abroad faster and farther. More and more people become his followers.

From Palestine to other lands in Asia, from Asia across the sea to Greece, from Greece to Rome, the story goes. The followers increase in spite of opposition and violence. Then comes victory over all who oppose. Years pass, centuries pass. Still the story is told, still the number of followers grows. From Rome through Europe, then across the Atlantic with our ancestors goes this story.

Finally the movement turns back to the East, to lands where it is not known, China, Japan, India and far-away islands in distant seas. So it continues today. Still we read his story and as the finest thing possible for us, we try to do the things he said. What brought all this to pass?

The answer can be given briefly. The friends of Jesus came to believe he was not dead but living again. They had laid the poor body in the tomb, but Jesus, the loving great spirit they had known, seemed to them to be alive. How did they know it? That is harder to say. Those who came to know this, the women who had been so loyal, Peter who had failed but was after all so loyal — these and others did somehow become sure that Jesus had made himself known to them. They said one to another, " He is alive."

They tried to tell how they knew it, but the thing was so great and wonderful they could not describe it. They spoke of angels coming to them, but we know

that angels are not real beings. We speak of them to
describe influences we do not quite understand. Some
said one thing, others said another. Their reports did
not quite agree. This always happens when people try
to tell of a wonderful thing they do not altogether understand. But on one thing they did agree. One thing
was sure, although they might be puzzled to explain
everything connected with it: Jesus was alive.

Because of that they grew brave and confident.
They came together. They told his story. They were
ready to die for him. Some did. All lived for him.
And his story was told. The Christian religion spread.

This little book is not to tell you the story of Chris-
tianity. Some day you will study it. We will not do
so now. But let me tell you of one other thing that
happened.

Jesus had spoken of what God was like. People
who heard about Jesus began to say: " He acts as God
would if he were on earth as a man. If we want to
know what God is like, we can think of Jesus."

This was a wonderful thing. No one has seen God.
We believe that he is an all-great, all-wise, all-kind
power. But how vague that is. Although you know
what all those words mean, perhaps that sentence does
not mean much to you. It is hard to think what God
is like until we say "He is like Jesus." No one who
ever lived has so clearly helped us to know God. Jesus
tells us what God is like as the sunshine falling on my

desk tells me what the sun is, or the water that I see
if I stand on the sandy shore tells me of the ocean.

Do you see, then, what a wonderful thing Jesus did
for the world? At different times great men have
made discoveries which have changed our way of
thinking and acting. You will recall some of these.
There was the man who found a way to print with
movable types and so enabled men to have books.
There was another man who thought of the steam
locomotive, and yet another of the steamboat. Then
there were the men who made the automobile and
telephone and radio possible. All such were great
men.

And yet, wonderful as these things are, the people
who use them may be just as mean and selfish and
thoughtless as those who lived before any of them
were discovered. What is needed most of all and all
the time is that we should be able to get the better of
our bad tempers, our foolish desires and our unkind
thoughts. Here is where Jesus was great and so was
greatest of all. By what he discovered about God he
helps us more than anyone else to have better and
nobler characters. For he shows us most of God and
God's care for us. Then because God is our Father,
we who are his children are brothers and sisters to
each other. And this gives us knowledge of the way
to live day by day.

Jesus made the greatest of all discoveries. He
taught the most useful of all truths. He gave us the

secret of the most difficult thing in the world. So men have loved and reverenced him. So he calls us all to follow him in his thought of God and his way of treating other people.

QUESTIONS AND TOPICS FOR STUDY

Why did Jesus' work not end at his death? Who helped carry it on? Had Jesus' faith in his friends proved to be justified?

How did the story of Jesus' life and teachings travel? Could you trace on your map where it started, how it went westward, and all over the globe? Why did this story live on? Why did Jesus' friends feel he was still with them? What effect did this have on their lives? How did it help the Christian religion to spread?

Why do many people feel that Jesus has helped them to know more about God? How can Jesus help us to have better and nobler characters? If God is the Father of us all, how should we act toward one another? Why?

What is the greatest of all discoveries ever made? If you discover something very important, what do you wish to do about it right away?

How can you share the story of Jesus and his discovery with somebody now? What is more important even than telling about it? Do you know how the present-day followers of Jesus help others, besides telling his story? List as many different ways as you can.

Further Discoveries

Read a story told about Jesus' teaching his friends after this. (Luke 24: 13-35.) What last message did the disciples say that Jesus gave them? (Matthew 28: 16-20.) What else did Jesus say about the work spreading? (Acts 1: 8.) Why do you think he told his disciples to preach in Samaria as well as in Judea? Who was one of the first to help spread the story of Jesus? (Acts 2: 14, 22, 23, 36-42.) Was Peter afraid now to say he knew Jesus? Why not? Read what he said to those who had tried to put Jesus to death. (Acts 3: 11-17; 4: 1-10, 13-20.)

Something to Do

How will you complete your diary? What maps should you like to include in it to explain its story? What pictures have you been able to find for it? What kind of cover would you like to make for this private Gospel of yours? Should you like to copy a poem or some part of a hymn inside the cover? What else can you do to make it fine? How will you make good use of this story?

Books for Further Reading

The Hidden Years, John Oxenham. Longmans, Green and Co., New York.
"Gentlemen—the King!" John Oxenham. Pilgrim Press, Boston and Chicago.
By An Unknown Disciple. Harper & Brothers, New York.
"The White Lily," an Easter story in *The Golden Goblet,* Jay T. Stocking. Pilgrim Press, Boston and Chicago.

Pictures to Study

From *Religion in Art, Series A: The Life of Christ,* Albert E. Bailey. Pilgrim Press.
The following numbers would be helpful: 7, 9, 13, 14, 15, 16, 20, 23, 24, 25, 26, 32, 33, 35, 37, 38, 50, 53, 60, 63, 65, 66, 70, 71, 72, 73, 74, 76, 89, 90, 91.

About half of these may also be procured from the Wilde Bible Pictures (131 Clarendon St., Boston, Mass.), but the Bailey set would be more valuable on account of the questions for study on the back of each picture.